The Beard & VKTMS

ALSO BY MICHAEL McCLURE

Plays
The Mammals
Gargoyle Cartoons
Gorf
The Grabbing of the Fairy
Josephine the Mouse Singer

Poetry
Hymns to Saint Geryon
Dark Brown
The New Book/A Book of Torture
Ghost Tantras
Star
September Blackberries
Rare Angel
Jaguar Skies
Antechamber
Fragments of Perseus

Essays
Meat Science Essays
Scratching the Beat Surface

Novels
The Mad Cub
The Adept

Biography
Freewheelin Frank Secretary of the Angels
—as told to Michael McClure

The Beard & VKTMS

Two Plays by Michael McClure

WITH A FOREWORD BY NORMAN MAILER

Grove Press, Inc./New York

First Grove Press Edition 1985
First Printing 1985
ISBN: 0-394-54132-4
Library of Congress Catalog Card Number: 84-48293

First Evergreen Edition 1985
First Printing 1985
ISBN: 0-394-62290-1
Library of Congress Catalog Card Number: 84-48293

Library of Congress Cataloging in Publication Data

McClure, Michael.
    The beard ; and, Vktms.

    I. McClure, Michael.   Vktms.   1985.   II. Title.
Beard.   III. Title: Vktms.
PS3563.A262A6   1985   812'.54   84-48293
ISBN 0-394-54132-4
ISBN 0-394-62290-1 (pbk.)

Printed in the United States of America

GROVE PRESS, INC., 196 West Houston Street, New York, N.Y. 10014

1   3   5   4   2

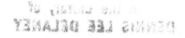

THE BEARD

THE BEARD

FOREWORD

Michael McClure's *The Beard* is a mysterious piece of work, for while its surface seems simple, repetitive and obscene, there is an action working which is dramatic and comic at once, and the play emits an odd but intense field of attention, almost like a magnetic field, almost as if ghosts from two periods of the American past were speaking across decades to each other, and yet at the same time are present in our living room undressing themselves or speaking to us of the nature of seduction, the nature of attraction, and particularly, the nature of perverse temper between a man and a woman. Obstinacy face to face with the sly feint and parry all in one, the repetition serves almost as subway stops on that electric trip a man and a woman make if they move from the mind to the flesh. That mysterious trip, whose mystery often resides in the dilemma of whether the action is extraordinarily serious or meaningless. It is with these ambiguities, these effervescences, that *The Beard* plays, masterfully, be it said, like a juggler.

—Norman Mailer

The Beard was performed for the first time on December 18, 1965 at the Actor's Workshop in San Francisco. The play was directed by Marc Estrin. The set was designed by Robert LaVigne and costumes were designed by Louise Foss. The cast was as follows:

JEAN HARLOW .... Billie Dixon
BILLY THE KID .... Richard Bright

The Beard was first published in a presentation edition of 300 copies.

It was subsequently published in a limited edition in March, 1967 by Coyote Books.

The author wishes to extend his special thanks to Billie Dixon, Richard Bright, Marc Estrin, Robert LaVigne, and Marshall Krause of the ACLU—for all we have gone through together to make a blue velvet eternity.

HARLOW *and* BILLY THE KID *wear small beards of torn white tissue paper.*

Harlow's hair is in her traditional style. She wears a pale blue gown with plumed sleeves.

BILLY THE KID *wears shirt, tight pants, and boots.*

HARLOW *has a purse.*

The set contains two chairs and a table covered with furs—there is an orange light shining on them.

HARLOW:
Before you can pry any secrets from me, you must first find the real me! Which one will you pursue?

THE KID:
What makes you think I want to pry secrets from you?

HARLOW:
Because I'm so beautiful.

THE KID:
So what!

HARLOW:
You want to be as beautiful as I am.

THE KID:
Oh yeah!

HARLOW:
Before you can pry any secrets from me, you must first find the real me! Which one will you pursue?

THE KID:

What makes you think I want to pry secrets from you?

HARLOW:

Because I'm so beautiful.

THE KID:

So what!

HARLOW:

You want to be as beautiful as I am.

THE KID:

Oh yeah! (*Pause. He grabs her arm.*)
I'VE GOT YOU!

HARLOW:

It's an illusion!

THE KID (*squeezing her arm and raising it*):
You mean this meat isn't you?

HARLOW:

What do you think?

THE KID:

What makes you think you're so beautiful?

HARLOW:

Oh, my thighs . . . my voice . . .

THE KID:

What about your hair . . . ?

HARLOW:

What do you think?

THE KID:

Your hair came out of a bottle.

8

HARLOW:

You're full of shit! My hair is beautiful and it didn't come out of any bottle—it's like this.

THE KID:

Show me your baby pictures!

HARLOW:

You're crazy! Why?

THE KID:

To see your hair!

HARLOW:

You ARE jealous.

THE KID:

You're full of shit!

HARLOW:

It's blond—don't worry! You've got buck teeth!

THE KID:

SHUT UP!

HARLOW:

You'd like to be beautiful! Maybe you'd even like to be pretty. You wear your hair down to your shoulders. Maybe you'd like to be a chick!

THE KID (*he takes hold of her arm—rolls it in his fingers*):

THIS IS NOTHING BUT MEAT! (*He sneers.*)

HARLOW:

Before you can pry any secrets from me, you must first find the real me!

THE KID:

What makes you think I want to pry secrets from you?

HARLOW:
Because I'm so beautiful.

THE KID:
So what!

HARLOW:
You want to be as beautiful as I am!

THE KID:
Oh yeah!
THIS IS NOTHING BUT MEAT! (*He squeezes her bare arm and rolls it in his fingers.*)—Why should I want to be beautiful?

HARLOW:
Oh . . . You're a man.

THE KID:
Yeah?

HARLOW:
You're a man . . . And men want to be beautiful.

THE KID:
I'm sick of that word . . . it makes me want to puke!
YOU'RE A BAG OF MEAT!

HARLOW:
What word?

THE KID:
Beautiful. I'm sick of hearing that word coming from a bag of meat.

HARLOW:
Don't touch my arm again!

THE KID:
Or?

HARLOW:

I'll cut your dumb brain open like a bag of meat!
—Don't you think I'm . . . lovely . . .

THE KID:

You smell like myrrh. Come and sit on my lap.
(*He pulls her arm.*)

HARLOW:

What if somebody came in and looked!

THE KID:

In eternity. —There's nobody here!

HARLOW:

You said I'm a bag of meat! And you said shit
about my hair!

THE KID:

Maybe I love you.

HARLOW:

You're full of shit. WHO CAN LOVE IN
ETERNITY?

THE KID (*with sureness*):
Sit on my lap.

HARLOW:

You're a million miles away, Sweet.

THE KID:

Not in eternity! . . . Sit on my lap!

HARLOW:

FUCK YOU!

THE KID:

YOU'RE A BAG OF MEAT! A white sack of soft
skin and fat held in shape by a lot of bones!

11

HARLOW (*pulling dress up thigh*):
So?

THE KID (*suddenly*):
I think your hair's blond!

HARLOW:
Really blond?

THE KID:
Yes!

HARLOW:
You're a sack of shit!

THE KID:
Sit on my lap!

HARLOW:
Before you can pry any secrets from me, you must first find the real me! Which one will you pursue?

THE KID:
What makes you think I want to pry secrets from you?

HARLOW:
Because I'm beautiful.

THE KID:
So what!

HARLOW:
You want to be as beautiful as I am!

THE KID:
Oh yeah! Come here, and sit on my lap and lick my boots!

12

HARLOW:

You're full of shit! You wish you were a chick!

THE KID:

Come here, and sit on my lap. I'll let you lick my boots.

HARLOW:

Why should I lick your boots?

THE KID:

You'd love to!

HARLOW:

Before you can pry any . . .

THE KID:

SHUT UP!

HARLOW:

You'd like to grab my blond hair in your hands?

THE KID:

So what!

HARLOW:

You'd like to see me crawl?

THE KID: (*shrugs.*)

HARLOW:

Why should I lick your boots?

THE KID (*shrugs*):

Come here and sit on my lap then.

HARLOW:

Why do you want me to lick your boots?

THE KID:

I'd like to make speeches like big thick clouds.

HARLOW:

You will, Baby, you will.

THE KID:

What if I talk like this—NICE AND LOUD!

HARLOW:

You want me to lick your boots, huh? That's no way to steal beauty, Kid.

THE KID:

Maybe I'll take your blond hair in my hands.

HARLOW:

Why don't you, Kid?

THE KID:

Come here and sit on my lap and lick my hands.

HARLOW:

Why don't you take me by the hair then?

THE KID:

Maybe I will.

Come over here and sit on my lap, Babe.

HARLOW:

One chick on another chick's lap? You're full of shit!

THE KID:

Before you can pry any secrets out of me, you must first find the real me! Which one will you pursue?

HARLOW:

What makes you think I want to pry secrets from you?

THE KID:

Because I'm beautiful.

14

HARLOW:

So what?

THE KID:

You want to be as beautiful as I am.

HARLOW:

You're nothing but meat pushed into a bag of skin with buck teeth and long hair. —And you want *me* to kiss YOUR boots.

THE KID:

Come here and sit on my lap and I'll let you hold my cock.

HARLOW:

Now wouldn't I like THAT! —A chunk of meat hanging from a hunk of meat!

THE KID:

And afterwards you can lick my boots! (—Which one of me will you pursue?) Maybe you'll find I'm sheer spirit taking the guise of meat.

HARLOW:

What makes you think I'd want to lick YOUR boots?

THE KID:

Because there are rainbows on them! Rainbows reflected on sheer black.

HARLOW:

Let me see.

THE KID: (*holds his boots in the light.*)

HARLOW:

They're not bad.

THE KID:

Come and sit on my lap.

HARLOW:

You're a cunt!

THE KID:

Sit on my lap.

HARLOW:

And you'll take my blond hair in your crumby hands! Why should I lick your boots or sit on your lap?

THE KID:

There's nobody here.

HARLOW:

Why should I lick your boots or sit on your lap?

THE KID:

THERE'S NOBODY HERE!

HARLOW:

Nobody to see, you mean? Huh?

THE KID:

That's right. There's nobody here. Sit on my lap.

HARLOW:

What if I DID?

THE KID:

You could lick my boots then . . . and touch my cock!

HARLOW:

You must first find the real me! Which one will you pursue?

THE KID:

There's only one you!

HARLOW:

You're full of shit! O.K., I'm sick of this! What do you want?

THE KID:

I want you to sit on my lap and touch my cock.

HARLOW:

I don't give a fuck where we are . . . I'm sick of this talk!

THE KID:

Then shut up! You started it!

HARLOW:

What I said was: Before you can pry any secrets out of me, you must first find the real me! Which one will you pursue?

THE KID:

I'm sick of this shit too! It's a fucking rite! It makes me think of one of those steel-black wasps crawling over blue velvet.

HARLOW:

And I suppose you're soft and real!

THE KID:

FUCK YOU!

HARLOW:

I'm real *wherever* I am!

THE KID (*sneering*):

Well, I'm real too.

17

HARLOW:

Your eyes are crazier than Hell! They stare! You're
out of your mind! Before you can pry any secrets
out of me, you must first find the real me! Which
one will you pursue?

THE KID:

I wouldn't follow you across an empty street.

HARLOW:

Well, you're HERE!

THE KID:

You're here too!
You say you're an illusion—and there's more than
one you! And you say my eyes are crazy! SHOVE
OFF!

HARLOW (*stands. Looks around*):

There's nothing here but blue velvet!

THE KID:

Yeah. (*Smiling, crossing leg.*)

(HARLOW *walks around stroking the velvet. Pauses.
Adjusts herself in the chair sexually.*)

THE KID:

What makes you say my eyes are crazy?

HARLOW:

I DON'T WANT TO TALK ABOUT IT. (*Pause.*)
Why do you say I'm an illusion?

THE KID:

You said it, not me!

HARLOW:

Yeah.

18

(*Thinking.*)
(*Pause.*)
Your eyes are crazy because you're full of shit,
Sweetie.

THE KID:
I despise dirty-mouthed chicks.

HARLOW:
Let's be clean . . .

THE KID:
O. K.

(*Pause.*)

HARLOW (*angrily*):
FUCK YOU!

(*Pause.* KID *takes out handkerchief and polishes
toes of his boots.*)

FUCK YOU! FUCK YOU! FUCK YOU!

(*Pause.* KID *polishes toes of his boots.*)

FUCK YOU! FUCK YOU! OHHhhh FUCK YOU!

THE KID:
And you say I'm crazy.

HARLOW:
You're crazier than Hell, you frozen eyed bastard!

THE KID:
Can't you be clean?

HARLOW:
How about you?

19

THE KID (*shrugs. Holds up his boot*):
How about that!

HARLOW:
You make me sick talking about your lap and your boots!

THE KID:
And my cock?

HARLOW:
That too! And calling me a bag of meat!

THE KID:
You said you were an illusion!

HARLOW:
Fuck you!

THE KID:
And you called me dumb and crazy.

HARLOW:
That was way back then in the rite.

THE KID:
Everything is NOW.

HARLOW:
You ARE crazy! (*Curls up in chair.*) I'm going to sleep . . .

THE KID:
In eternity?

HARLOW:
Skip it! (*Makes herself more comfortable.*)

(*Pause.*)

THE KID:
   Hey!

HARLOW:
   I'm asleep!

THE KID:
   Come and sit on my lap.

   (*No action.*)

   Hey!

   (*No action.*)

   Hey!

HARLOW (*leaping up*):
   YOU'RE OUT OF YOUR MIND!

THE KID:
   In eternity? (*Squinting.*) How can I be out of my
   mind in eternity?

HARLOW:
   If eternity is blue velvet it's a bunch of shit!
   (*Paces.*)

THE KID:
   Maybe it's not!

HARLOW (*pacing*):
   Not what?

THE KID:
   Velvet! (*Watches her pace.*)
   Sit down!

HARLOW:
   WHAT?

21

THE KID:
   Sit down.

HARLOW (*angrily*):
   In your lap?

THE KID (*quietly and firmly with a gesture*):
   Sit down.

   (HARLOW *sits back down in chair. —They stare at each other.*)

HARLOW (*enticingly*):
   Before you can pry any secrets from me, you must first find the real me! Which one will you pursue?

THE KID:
   SHUT UP!

HARLOW:
   Before you can pry any . . .

THE KID (*leaping up as if to strike her*):
   SHUT UP!

HARLOW:
   Before you can pry any . . .

THE KID (*raising hand to strike her*):
   SHUT UP!! SHUT UP!! GOD DAMN YOU! SHUT UP!

HARLOW (*putting hand over mouth*):
   Ho hum. (*Stretches.*) Ho hum. Ho hum. Ho . . . Ho . . . HOoooooooooooo . . . Ho hum.
   (*Looking directly at* KID.) Sit down you dumb fuck!

(THE KID *sits down again, hands on his knees, staring at* HARLOW. *Long pause.*)

THE KID (*serious/concentrated*):
> We can do anything we want to do here . . .
> There's nobody around to watch.

HARLOW (*stretching languorously*):
> Just like grownups, huh?

THE KID (*leaning toward her*):
> There's no one to watch.

HARLOW (*stretching more luxuriously*):
> No one can see us, huh?

THE KID:
> That's right.

HARLOW:
> What do you want to do?

THE KID:
> Just what I said.

HARLOW:
> That's what you want ME to do.

THE KID:
> That's right!

HARLOW:
> Sit on a tack!

THE KID:
> You know that's what you'd like to do . . .

HARLOW:
> Sit on your lap and play with your cock?

THE KID:

Yeah!

HARLOW (*stretching*):

OOOOOoooooh . . . (*Stretching arms.*) Ho . . .
Ho . . . Ho humm. You're out of your nut!

THE KID:

There's nobody here, Baby!

HARLOW:

So what!
Let me sleep. (*Curls up.*)

(*Pause.* HARLOW *feigns sleep.*)

THE KID:

I don't want to pry any secrets from you.

HARLOW:

I was just talking . . . That's all right.

THE KID:

I really don't.

HARLOW (*sleepily*):

It's all right.

THE KID:

What shall we do?

HARLOW:

Sleep.

THE KID:

No! WE'RE ABSOLUTELY FREE!

HARLOW (*sleepily*):

Shut up!

THE KID:

This is perfect liberty! (*Pause.*) We're divine!

HARLOW:

Sure . . . Sure . . .

THE KID:

Listen . . .

HARLOW:

You're out of your nut!

THE KID:

We're DIVINE!

HARLOW:

Sure . . . Sure . . .
I've always known it. (*Feigning sleep.*)

THE KID:

You're not asleep.

HARLOW:

Sure I am. I talk in my sleep!

THE KID:

I know you're a real blonde.

HARLOW:

I know you're crazy and full of shit.
Let me sleep!

THE KID:

You're great! There's only one you.

HARLOW:

Sure . . . But I'm asleep.

THE KID:

I like you asleep!

HARLOW:

God damn you, shut up!

THE KID:

    I'll take off your shoes . . . (*Starting to kneel.*)

HARLOW (*sitting up*):

    Keep away from my feet! (*Shaking head.*) You
    are a creepy bastard aren't you!

THE KID:

    We're DIVINE!

HARLOW:

    Oh yeah! Yeah . . . Yeah . . .

THE KID:

    YOU'RE A REAL BLONDE!

HARLOW:

    Sure.

THE KID:

    We're divine. We're in eternity!

HARLOW:

    Sure.

THE KID:

    I'm not trying to pry secrets from you.

HARLOW:

    I read that someplace.

THE KID:

    What?

HARLOW:

    That thing.

THE KID:

    Where.

HARLOW:
Where what?

THE KID:
Where did you read it?

HARLOW:
In a comic book.

THE KID (*angrily*):
Yeah!
Where did you read it?

HARLOW:
IN A COMIC BOOK!

THE KID:
OH YEAH!

HARLOW:
O.K., maybe I didn't.
Before you can pry any secrets from me you must
first . . .

THE KID:
Shut up!

HARLOW:
All right!

THE KID:
Listen, WE'RE DIVINE!

HARLOW:
Sure! Divinity is blue velvet!

THE KID:
And blond hair.

HARLOW:
And buck teeth!

THE KID:
    —Where did you read it?

HARLOW:
    I made it up!

THE KID:
    Oh yeah! Where did you read it?

HARLOW:
    I made it up!

THE KID:
    Sure!

HARLOW:
    I THOUGHT OF IT!

THE KID:
    Oh yeah!

HARLOW:
    You bet your ass I did! —Or maybe I read it.

THE KID:
    I'll bet you got fat laying on your ass reading comic books.

HARLOW:
    And eating chocolate goodies.

THE KID:
    Fuck you!

HARLOW:
    FUCK YOU!
    You call *me* fat—you dumb, creepy, bucktoothed bastard!

THE KID:
    Maybe that's divine! —Buck teeth, dumb, creepy.

HARLOW:

Maybe *divine* is nothing but blue velvet!

THE KID:

What comic book?

HARLOW:

It wasn't in a magazine! —Go to Hell!

THE KID:

Say it again!

HARLOW:

My God! My God!

THE KID:

SAY IT AGAIN!

HARLOW:

Ohh!

THE KID:

Again!

HARLOW:

OHH!

THE KID:

Again!

HARLOW:

Before you can pry any secrets . . .

THE KID:

You're not fat!

HARLOW:

Oh YEAH!

THE KID:

Listen, WE'RE DIVINE!

HARLOW:

I wouldn't listen to you shit in a rainbarrel!

THE KID:

We're divine, Baby, we're DIVINE!
This is really it. We're really here!

HARLOW:

Sure.

THE KID:

I mean it!

HARLOW:

Sure you mean it! You're crazier than fuck!

THE KID:

Oh yeah! Come here and sit on my lap and lick
my boots!

HARLOW:

You're full of it! You aren't even a man. You wish
you were a chick!

THE KID:

Come here and sit on my lap. —And lick my boots.

HARLOW:

Why should I lick your boots?

THE KID:

You'd love to!

HARLOW:

You'd like to grab my blond hair in your hands!

THE KID:

So what!

HARLOW:

You'd like to see me crawl?

THE KID: (*shrugs.*)

HARLOW:

Why should I lick your boots?

THE KID:

Come here and sit on my lap.

HARLOW:

Why do you want me to lick your boots?

THE KID:

Because we're divine, Babe, divine, and there's nobody here!

HARLOW:

Nobody to watch, huh?

THE KID:

That's right.

HARLOW:

What if I DID?

THE KID:

Then you could touch my cock.

HARLOW:

Just like grownups, huh?
You're full of shit!

THE KID:

We're divine!

HARLOW:

Sure!

THE KID:

I'm divine.

HARLOW:

And I suppose you think I'm not!

THE KID:

Yeah. Come and sit on my lap and I'll give you a shot . . .

HARLOW:

Not with that rod of yours—you'll make me laugh!

THE KID:

And you can lick my boots!

HARLOW:

What makes you think I want to sit on your lap or lick your boots?

THE KID:

There's nobody here!

HARLOW:

You mean people want to do it because there's nobody around?

THE KID:

Sure!

HARLOW:

What's so great about your boots?

THE KID:

Rainbows reflected on sheer black!

HARLOW:

O.K., what if I sit on your lap?

THE KID:

And touch my cock?

HARLOW:

My God!

32

THE KID:

My bare cock with your hand!

HARLOW:

I'm going to go to sleep!

THE KID:

God damn you!

HARLOW:

You've got a dirty mouth!
(*Pause.*)
What did you mean when you said I'm an illusion?

THE KID:

I didn't say it—you did. I said you're a bag of meat!

HARLOW:

Then what's so great about me? —What do you want with a bag of meat? (Before you can pry any secrets from me, you must first find the real me! Which one will you pursue?)
What do you mean—bag of meat?

THE KID:

Why don't you find the real you and pursue it yourself!

HARLOW:

Screw you!

THE KID:

Come over here and sit on my lap!

HARLOW:

All right there's nobody here. So what!
(*Pause. No action.* HARLOW *curls herself up.*)
I'm going to sleep.

33

THE KID:
    A bag of meat is a bag of meat!

HARLOW: (*sits bolt upright.*)

THE KID:
    Stuffed with fat and bones!

HARLOW:
    You're a pain in the ass!

THE KID:
    In eternity?

HARLOW:
    Sure, wherever you are!

THE KID:
    Good night!

HARLOW:
    Fuck you!
    You're a prim little cunt for a tough guy!

THE KID:
    A bag of meat is a bag of meat!

HARLOW (*pulls dress up leg*):
    Look at that!

THE KID:
    Come and sit on my lap!

HARLOW:
    For Christ sake!

THE KID:
    What makes you think I want to pry secrets from
    you?

34

HARLOW:
  You don't interest me!

THE KID:
  Not in eternity?

HARLOW:
  Not even in eternity!

THE KID:
  I'll bet!

HARLOW:
  That's right!

THE KID:
  You're lying.

  (*Pause.* HARLOW *feigns sleep.*)

  Hey!
  You're a NICE bag of meat!

HARLOW:
  For Christ sake!

THE KID:
  I like your leg.

HARLOW:
  It's a bag of meat.

THE KID:
  Yeah.

HARLOW:
  So?

THE KID:
  I like a nice bag of meat.

35

HARLOW:

You're a crude S.O.B.

THE KID:

And buck toothed?

HARLOW:

With your hair hanging halfway down to your
crack like a floozie!

THE KID:

Before you can pry any secrets from me, you must
first find the real me! Which one will you pursue?

HARLOW:

Shit!

THE KID:

Before you can pry any . . .

HARLOW:

Shit!

THE KID:

Before you can pry any secrets from me, you must
first find the real me . . .

HARLOW:

O.K., who are you?

THE KID:

Blue velvet.

HARLOW:

That's an illusion. You look like a hunk of meat.

THE KID:

Sit on my lap!

HARLOW:

And I suppose I'm supposed to be blond hair—like blond hair on blue velvet?

THE KID:

Suit yourself!

HARLOW:

O.K., together we're blond hair on blue velvet.

THE KID:

That's not enough.

HARLOW:

What's not enough?

THE KID:

Blond hair on blue velvet!

HARLOW:

I suppose because there's nobody around there should be something more?

THE KID:

Yeah!

HARLOW:

Like what?

THE KID:

Like . . .

HARLOW:

—Sit on a tack!

THE KID:

It's not a tack you'd like to sit on.

HARLOW:

Yeah!

THE KID:

    It's something else.

HARLOW:

    Like what? Your lap?

THE KID:

    You're close!

HARLOW:

    Awhh!

    (*Pause.*)

THE KID:

    Blond hair on blue velvet isn't enough!
    Maybe I love you.

HARLOW:

    What's love!
    You're jealous of my beauty!

THE KID:

    I don't give a fuck about your beauty! If I wanted
    you I'd want YOU!

HARLOW:

    Oh yeah?
    I'm sick of hearing about your boots!

THE KID:

    When I say *boots* I don't mean boots.

HARLOW:

    What do you mean then?

THE KID:

    When I say blond hair and blue velvet I don't
    mean that either.

HARLOW:

What do you mean then?

THE KID:

By boots?

HARLOW:

Yeah, by boots.

THE KID:

I don't give a fuck about beauty! If I wanted you
I'd want YOU!

HARLOW:

You said that. What do you mean by boots?

THE KID:

My cock!

HARLOW:

Oh my God!

THE KID:

MY COCK!

HARLOW:

I'm going to look at the walls. (HARLOW *walks
stroking walls.*)
They're nice!

THE KID:

I'm your walls!

HARLOW:

Shit! (*Pause.*)
What do you mean I'm fat?

THE KID:

I said you're a real blonde!

(Pause.)
I'm your walls to rub against.

HARLOW:
    HERE?

THE KID:
    Anywhere!

HARLOW:
    They're soft.

THE KID:
    I'm soft too.
    And hard as a rock!

HARLOW (*walks looking at walls and stroking them.
    Looks directly at* KID):
    Bullshit!
    Before you can pry any secrets from me, you must
    first find the real me!

THE KID:
    Yeah!

HARLOW:
    Find it!

THE KID:
    Sit on my lap and stroke my cock!

HARLOW:
    You're a fucking monomaniac!

THE KID:
    And lick my boots.

HARLOW:
    You said it wasn't your boots!
    . . . Never mind!

40

THE KID:

Sit on my lap . . .

HARLOW:

And touch your cock?

THE KID:

There's nobody here!

HARLOW:

Just like grownups, huh?
Why isn't blond hair on blue velvet enough?

THE KID:

Because you're a bag of meat!

HARLOW:

I'm an illusion.
What do you mean you'd want ME?
Why isn't blond hair on blue velvet enough?

THE KID:

Because you're a bag of meat!

HARLOW:

I'm a real BLONDE!

THE KID:

That's what I said.

HARLOW:

You wanted to see my baby pictures.

THE KID:

I believed it!

HARLOW:

Why do you want ME?

THE KID:

Because you're here!

HARLOW:

Fuck you!

THE KID:

That's the price you pay!

HARLOW:

What? What price?

THE KID:

The price for being here.

HARLOW:

Piss!

THE KID:

Piss on you!

HARLOW:

You ARE JEALOUS of my beauty!

THE KID:

We're DIVINE, Babe, divine!

HARLOW:

Well, what the Hell does that mean?

THE KID:

We're DIVINE, Babe, divine!

HARLOW:

Well, what the Hell does that mean?

THE KID:

We're HERE!

HARLOW:

If being HERE is divine it's a bunch of shit! Maybe I don't even like it here . . . looking at your crazy eyes, and buck teeth and long hair!

And hearing all of that crap about blond hair and
blue velvet! Besides you're an ugly fucker! You
aren't even my type!

THE KID:

You wouldn't know divine from a handful of shit.
You're here by accident!

HARLOW:

If you're divine it's a big mistake!
If you're divine I'd rather be elsewhere!

THE KID:

Lying on a bed with a magazine?

HARLOW:

Yeah.

THE KID:

You'd be divine there too.

HARLOW:

You said I wouldn't know divine from a handful
of shit!

THE KID:

You wouldn't know it but you'd be there!

HARLOW:

WHERE?

THE KID:

Here!

HARLOW:

Where's here?

THE KID:

Where we're divine!

HARLOW:

I wouldn't be divine with you on a bet! You're full of shit and you're a God damn monomaniac bore!

THE KID:

What about my cock?

HARLOW:

Ohhh!

THE KID:

I can't help that I'm divine. I didn't plan it. I'm HERE! —I *decided* it.

HARLOW:

Decided what?

THE KID:

I decided it—but I didn't plan it!

HARLOW:

Decided what?

THE KID:

To be HERE—to be divine!

HARLOW:

. . . CRAP! What do you mean *I'm* here by accident? I thought it out every step of the way.

THE KID:

Then you wanted to be with me!

HARLOW:

You're full of it—and I'm sick of hearing you. —I *planned* it!

THE KID:

Planned what?

44

HARLOW:

Being here. Being divine. Being wherever I am with blond hair!

THE KID:

Then you wanted to be with ME!
I decided it—and it happened.

HARLOW:

Then you wanted to be with *me*!

THE KID:

I never even heard of you!

HARLOW:

How did you make it happen?

THE KID:

By deciding it—deciding to be divine.

HARLOW:

And we're here together.

THE KID:

That's right!

HARLOW:

Before you can pry any secrets from me, you must first find the real me! Which one will you pursue?

THE KID:

You're a nice bag of meat!

HARLOW:

For Christ sake!

THE KID:

I like your leg.

HARLOW:
It's a bag of meat.

THE KID:
Yeah.

HARLOW:
So?

THE KID:
I like a nice bag of meat.

HARLOW:
And we're divine!

THE KID:
And we're free, this is liberty, and there's nobody here!

HARLOW:
It's always that way.

THE KID:
That's what I mean!

HARLOW:
O.K., this is liberty, we're free, and there's nobody here . . . So . . . ?

THE KID:
Sit on my lap and touch my cock.

HARLOW:
And what about your boots?

THE KID:
Forget that. I'll kneel and kiss your feet.

HARLOW:
You already tried that.

THE KID:

Yes.

I'll do it again. (*Starting to kneel.*)

HARLOW (*pulling feet back*):

The fuck you will!

(*Pause.*) You know, you look like you're blind. Or maybe crazy, or angry. You're out of your mind. No, not blind . . . something else . . .

THE KID:

I'm seeing everywhere.

HARLOW:

Yeah?

THE KID:

You are too.

HARLOW:

O.K., we're seeing everywhere in liberty, huh?

THE KID:

Sure.

I'll take off your shoes!

HARLOW:

Get away! I'm here because I planned it and I'll do what I please.

THE KID:

I'm not raping you.

HARLOW:

Yeah?

(*Pause.*)

What do you mean you're here because you decided?

47

THE KID:

I decided to be divine—and you're divine too.

HARLOW:

So what! I didn't ask for you!

THE KID:

Nor did I ask for you—but we're blond hair on blue velvet.

HARLOW:

You said that wasn't it—blond hair on blue velvet isn't it!

THE KID:

It's not. It's something more.

HARLOW:

Like?

THE KID:

Like being a bag of meat and being divine in liberty.

HARLOW (*angrily*):

With your hair down to your crack!

THE KID:

Sure. Sit on my lap and I'll show you how.

HARLOW:

How what?

THE KID:

How to be divine!

HARLOW:

I'm so divine I'm free of you and all your shit.

THE KID:

Nobody's free of being divine!

HARLOW:

O.K., I'M SICK OF ALL THIS SHIT AND I'M TIRED OF HEARING YOU RAVE ABOUT *DIVINE* AND *LIBERTY!* You tricked me into talking with you.

THE KID:

YOU DON'T HAVE ANY CHOICE—you're here, and you're divine and free, and you're going to sit on my lap and touch my cock. You're going to listen because you're free, and you're going to do what I tell you! And we're going to do a lot more too. And if you don't (then) I'm going to do it all to you. AND YOU'RE GOING TO TAKE ALL THAT SHIT ABOUT ME BEING A CUNT AND YOU'RE GOING TO SWALLOW IT UP YOUR DIRTY ASS AGAIN!

HARLOW:

LISTEN, YOU LITTLE FUCKER, YOU MAY RAPE ME BUT . . .

THE KID:

I WOULDN'T TOUCH YOU!

HARLOW:

You wouldn't, huh?

THE KID:

Not till you ask.

HARLOW:

I'll never ask!

THE KID:

Not till you're willing!

HARLOW:

You just threatened me with rape!

THE KID:

Yeah! But I wouldn't touch you with a long stick!

HARLOW (*taking deep breath*):
O.K., what's *divine*?

THE KID:

Divine is free!

HARLOW:

And there's nobody here? AND WE'RE BAGS
OF MEAT?

THE KID:

You're a bag of meat!

HARLOW:

And what are you?

THE KID:

I am too—and something more!

HARLOW:

Like what?
—You wouldn't dare touch me!

THE KID:

I'd dare—but I wouldn't!

HARLOW:

YOU'RE SCARED!

THE KID:

Hmm!

(KID *grabs* HARLOW *and wrestles with her.*)

HARLOW:
GOD DAMN YOU! LET LOOSE OF ME YOU
DIRTY FUCKER!
GOD DAMN YOU! OH! OH! GOD DAMN
YOU!!

(THE KID *gets Harlow's shoes off and bites her foot.*
HARLOW *screams.*)

(*Gritting teeth.*) Oh, you dirty fucker! You dirty
God damn son of a bitch. . . . I think it's bleeding.
(*She holds up foot to look at it closely.*)

THE KID: (*turns his back on* HARLOW. *Goes and looks
at the velvet walls.*)

HARLOW:
YOU TORE MY STOCKING! YOU TORE MY
STOCKING WITH YOUR TEETH! YOU TORE
MY STOCKING WITH YOUR ROTTEN
TEETH!

THE KID (*sneeringly*):
Yeah, that's *divine!*

HARLOW (*nursing her foot*):
Now you are being a cunt—with that silly sneer.
Oh, my poor foot!
You are a crazy bastard! Biting a woman's foot!
Look what you did to my stocking! —I think there's
some blood! Oh, my God, there's going to be
blood!

THE KID:
Quit squeezing it.

HARLOW:
  I'm going to be sick.

THE KID:
  The Hell you are!

HARLOW:
  Blood makes me sick.

THE KID:
  Baloney!
  Quit squeezing it!

HARLOW:
  Look at my stocking! Look at that tear!

THE KID:
  Take your stockings off!

HARLOW (*squintingly*):
  No telling where you'd bite me then.

THE KID:
  Come here and sit on my lap.

HARLOW:
  You crazy, crazy bastard—I don't know why we
  have to be HERE!
  (*Squeezing.*) Oh, my God, there's blood!

THE KID:
  Let me see!

HARLOW:
  What are you, a fucking vampire? Get away from
  me! Get away you son of a bitch! Get away from
  me or I'll . . .

THE KID:
  Scream?

HARLOW:

I wouldn't scream—I can take care of you.

THE KID:

Why wouldn't you scream?— Because you want to be *here*?

HARLOW (*squeezing*):

Fuck you!— Look there's some blood!

THE KID:

Where?

HARLOW:

Right by the toe. (*Pointing.*)

THE KID:

Do you like it?

HARLOW:

Are you kidding?

THE KID:

You squeezed it.

HARLOW:

My God, I can't stand blood.

THE KID:

You feel faint?

HARLOW:

You sadist!

THE KID:

Sit on my lap!

HARLOW:

You're crazier than a hoot owl. You threw me

53

down and bit my foot like some fucking Jack the Ripper maniac!

THE KID:

You liked it.

HARLOW:

You're full of shit! (*Studies toe.*) Look at that! You like the blood. There, take a good look at it! (*Stretching tear with her finger.*) Look at that— Where's my comb? (*Combs hair.*)

THE KID:

I like your breasts too.

HARLOW (*sneeringly*):

It's about time you noticed them. That makes me very happy! I suppose you'd like to draw blood out of them too! I suppose you'd like to bite the nipples off—you sadist pervert!

THE KID:

You asked me to.

HARLOW:

To what—bite my tits off?

THE KID:

To put you in your place.

HARLOW:

I suppose biting a woman on the foot puts her in her place? You make me laugh!
Look at that ruined stocking you fucking creep!

THE KID:

It looks good! I'm beginning to want you.

HARLOW:

Isn't that romantic! (*Taking mirror.*) Get out of the light!

THE KID:

What do you see?

HARLOW:

If you'd get out of the light I'd see something besides your fucking shadow!

THE KID:

I like your breasts.

HARLOW:

So does everybody! (*Pause.*) Is everybody divine?

THE KID:

Before you can pry any secrets from me, you must first find the real me!

HARLOW:

Fuck off! (*Combing hair again.*)
(*Angrily:*) Look at that stocking!
(*Pause. Thoughtful.*)
Do you think everybody is divine?

THE KID:

How should I know?

HARLOW:

What do you *think*?

THE KID:

Sure!

HARLOW:

I don't!

THE KID:
Don't what?

HARLOW:
Think they're divine!

THE KID:
Yeah?

HARLOW:
STAY A GOOD LONG DISTANCE AWAY
FROM ME!

THE KID:
Why not?

HARLOW:
Maybe they are . . .

THE KID:
Are what?

HARLOW:
Divine. Maybe they're divine and don't know it!

THE KID:
That's what I'm trying to tell *you*.

HARLOW:
Yeah, by biting my poor foot till it bleeds . . .

THE KID:
You squeezed it till it bled.

HARLOW:
And ruining my stocking!

THE KID:
You called me a cunt!

HARLOW:

Yeah? Maybe I'm sorry.
(*Pause.*)
And maybe I'm not!

THE KID:

Take off your stockings!

HARLOW:

—Maybe you'd like to see my tits too?

THE KID:

Sure.

HARLOW:

You make me laugh!

THE KID:

Take off your stockings.

HARLOW:

You'd probably lick the blood right off my toe.

THE KID:

Maybe I would if I could find it.

HARLOW:

What do you mean, if you could find it! IT'S
THERE! Right there! Look! (*Puts her leg up on
the chair.*) There it is right by my toe! Right on
the fucking stocking you've ruined!

THE KID: (*puts his hand on her thigh.*)

HARLOW:

GET YOUR HAND OFF, YOU CRUMBY
BASTARD!
If you ever touch me I'll kill you—you . . .

57

THE KID:
   Cunt?

HARLOW:
   You filthy sadist . . . (*Struggling for words.*)

THE KID:
   Listen, Baby, we're divine . . .

HARLOW:
   FOR CHRIST SAKE!
   —Look at that stocking—it's wiped out!

THE KID:
   Take it off then. Be divine!

HARLOW:
   Who's afraid to be divine! If taking off my stocking is divine then you're a creep!

THE KID:
   It's divine to you—not to me!

HARLOW:
   You're the one who'll get the kick!

THE KID:
   It'll be your act!

HARLOW:
   Whataya mean my *act*?

THE KID:
   Your DEED!

HARLOW:
   Taking off my stocking will be my divine deed?

THE KID:
   Yeah!

HARLOW:

O.K.! (*Takes off stocking. Holds it up.*) LOOK
AT THAT!

THE KID:

I'm watching you be divine.

HARLOW:

SHIT!
—I could put my arm through that tear!

THE KID:

You stretched it. Picking and tearing for blood.

HARLOW:

YOU RUINED MY STOCKING!

THE KID:

Yeah. So?

HARLOW:

You ugly rat!

THE KID:

HUH! (*Indifferently.*)

HARLOW:

I suppose it doesn't matter because we're divine!

THE KID:

That's right!

HARLOW:

What's a stocking in eternity, huh?

THE KID:

Yeah, what's a stocking in eternity, huh? (*Mock-ing.*)

HARLOW (*nursing foot*):
    And what's a toe?

THE KID:
    That's right.

HARLOW:
    Well, it's my toe! What if I bit yours?

THE KID:
    Go ahead! (*Smiles.*)

HARLOW:
    You silly shit!

THE KID:
    I can be crazy and divine, or silly and divine—or
    violent and divine!

HARLOW:
    I could too!

THE KID:
    Then why don't you?

HARLOW:
    Look at that toe. The stocking is completely
    ruined . . .
    How?

THE KID:
    Sit on my lap and . . .

HARLOW:
    SHUT . . .

THE KID:
    You're divine!!

60

HARLOW:
UP!

THE KID:
Stop!

HARLOW (*cynically*):
All right. (*Standing one foot on chair holding stocking up.*)

THE KID:
One bare leg—in a pale dress—you're holding an empty stocking up—your blond hair is a crown, it's an emblem of eternity—there's blood on your bare foot—your hair is mussed, there's anger in your eyes and you're aroused!

HARLOW:
You're fucking right I am!

THE KID:
SHUT UP!
One bare leg—in a pale dress—you're holding an empty stocking up—it hangs in the light . . .

HARLOW:
ISN'T THAT POETIC!

THE KID:
Moist from your thighs . . .

HARLOW:
From wrestling with you, you dumb fuck!

THE KID:
YOU'RE REAL NOW!

61

HARLOW:

OF COURSE I AM—THAT SLOBBER DOESN'T
MAKE ME MORE REAL!

THE KID:

BUT BITING DID!

HARLOW:

FUCK YOU!

THE KID:

Take the other one off!

HARLOW:

Shit.

THE KID:

Take it off!

HARLOW:

Maybe I will. I look like a fool with one stocking
on and one off. (*She begins to take it off.*)

THE KID:

There's nobody here to watch.

HARLOW:

Nobody to see me be a fool, huh? (*Pauses with
stocking.*)
I thought you wanted me to take it off.
What do you mean biting my foot made me real?

THE KID:

It makes me real—not you.

HARLOW:

We're both real—skip it. (*Taking stocking off.*)

THE KID:
Which one of you will I pursue.

HARLOW:
Fuck off!

THE KID:
Which one?

HARLOW:
There's only one me!

THE KID:
What?

HARLOW:
One me! There's only one ME!

THE KID:
Bull shit!

HARLOW:
Whataya mean?

THE KID:
You convinced me otherwise.

HARLOW:
Otherwise than what?

THE KID:
That there's more than one you!

HARLOW:
Jesus, that toe still hurts!

THE KID:
Which one is divine?

63

HARLOW:
Look at that tooth mark!

THE KID:
Yeah.
Which one is divine?

HARLOW:
I'M DIVINE!

THE KID:
Sure, I've heard that before.

HARLOW:
I'm divine you son of a bitch—and you're divine too!

THE KID:
Yeah!

HARLOW:
And you're after my beauty!

THE KID:
What beauty?

HARLOW:
My blond beauty!

THE KID:
I'm only after *my* beauty!

HARLOW:
You're a weird fuck!

THE KID:
We're in Heaven.

HARLOW:
It's a heaven full of tooth marks then!

THE KID:

This IS HEAVEN!

HARLOW:

You're only after my beauty!

THE KID:

Take off your pants!

HARLOW:

WHAT!

THE KID:

Take off your pants!

HARLOW:

Maybe I will! Maybe I just will to see what you do.

(HARLOW *takes off her pants.*)

THE KID:

Hand them to me.

HARLOW:

You're crazy!

THE KID:

Hand them to me.

HARLOW:

You're out of your nut!

(THE KID *takes the panties from* HARLOW *who stands staring at him.*)

HARLOW:

Give them back you fucker!

THE KID:

They're warm.

HARLOW:

What did you expect—ice?

THE KID:

And they're moist.

HARLOW:

You expect sand? Now give them back!

THE KID: (*He tears them in half.*)

HARLOW (*gasping with astonishment*):

YOU'RE CRAZY!

(*Picking up the pieces.*) My poor panties. My God, My God.

THE KID:

Sit on my lap!

HARLOW:

YOU'RE A FUCKING MANIAC! You're a raving drooling MURDERER!

THE KID:

We're divine and we're flesh and blood and anything else is shit! IF WE DON'T DO WHAT WE WANT WE'RE NOT DIVINE! WHAT DO YOU WANT?

HARLOW:

I don't know!

THE KID:

What do you want?

HARLOW:

My God, my clothes! Oh, my poor clothes!

THE KID:

What do you want?

HARLOW:

SHUT UP! SHUT UP! LOOK AT THESE FUCK-
ING RAGS! YOU'VE BITTEN ME AND TORN
UP MY CLOTHES! WHAT IN THE HELL IS
HAPPENING. Where are we? Who the Hell are
you? Who am I? Look at my fucking clothes . . .
my clothes . . . And my God damn hair! Where's
my comb?
—Why did you do that?

THE KID:

I wanted to.

HARLOW (*shaking head and backing away*): You're
violent—and you're crazy!

THE KID:

You don't need clothes in eternity except for
decoration.— A toothmark goes away in Heaven or
Hell. You don't need anything to perpetuate illusion. I don't want your beauty or any other—
I only want to enact mine.

HARLOW:

YOU'RE ALMOST BEAUTIFUL!

THE KID:

Yeah.

HARLOW:

You're too fucking dumb to talk but you're almost
beautiful.

THE KID:

It's like a vision . . .

HARLOW:

That's a dumb word.

67

THE KID:
What?

HARLOW:
Vision—vision is a dumb word.

THE KID:
What if I said you're as beautiful as a vision!

HARLOW:
It sounds better then.

THE KID:
Sit on my lap.

HARLOW:
YOU'RE OUT OF YOUR MIND! Before you can pry any secrets out of me you must first find the real me!

THE KID:
I already have!

HARLOW:
Where?

THE KID:
THERE! (*Points to panties on the floor.*)

HARLOW:
You're full of shit. THAT'S NOT ME! That's a pair of torn panties!

THE KID:
What's you then?

HARLOW:
ME . . . HERE . . . ME . . .

THE KID:

A BAG OF MEAT!

HARLOW:

YEAH! A BAG OF MEAT!

THE KID:

Swirling in eternity?

HARLOW:

Yeah, swirling in eternity! Or solid HERE—it doesn't make any difference!

THE KID:

Is that what you want?

HARLOW:

Yeah!

THE KID:

Are you sure?

HARLOW:

I planned it!

THE KID:

What did you plan?

HARLOW:

To be in eternity!

THE KID:

How did you plan it.

HARLOW:

By doing what I want!

THE KID:

That's called destiny!

HARLOW:

To do what you want?

THE KID:

Yeah!

HARLOW:

I guess you said it!
What it is . . . Destiny.
—I DON'T WANT TO TALK TO YOU! YOU
TORE UP MY PANTIES!

THE KID:

In eternity?

HARLOW:

Yeah, you tore up my panties in eternity! Or any
other fucking place. You tore up my pants!

THE KID:

And you called me a cunt!

HARLOW:

Yeah, I called you a cunt!

THE KID:

In eternity!

HARLOW:

Yeah, I called you a cunt in eternity!

THE KID:

Come here and sit on my lap.

HARLOW:

You're out of your mind!

THE KID:

What do you want?

70

HARLOW:

I want to stand here and comb my hair—while I figure what to do about you.

THE KID:

What do you want to do?

HARLOW:

Will you shut up!— I'm combing my hair!

THE KID:

You're combing your blond hair in eternity and you don't know what to do there!

HARLOW:

Yeah!

THE KID:

And you planned to be there?

HARLOW:

Where?

THE KID:

Here.

HARLOW:

Yeah!
—And you decided to be here?

THE KID:

Yeah.

HARLOW:

How did you decide?

THE KID:

By doing what I wanted to do.

HARLOW:

And that's called destiny?

THE KID:

Yeah, it's only a word. People call destiny doing what you want to do.

HARLOW:

What the bag of meat tells you to do?

THE KID:

Yeah.

HARLOW:

What does your bag of meat tell you to do?

THE KID:

To get you on my lap.

HARLOW:

And that's why you tore up my panties and bit my toe?

THE KID:

—I did what I wanted to do.

HARLOW:

What if that was what I want you to do?

THE KID:

It's the same thing—it doesn't matter.

HARLOW:

WHY NOT?

THE KID:

We want the same thing and (we) enact it between us.

HARLOW:
> BULLSHIT!

THE KID:
> What?

HARLOW:
> Just bullshit!
> —What do you mean "between us"?

THE KID:
> RIGHT HERE!

HARLOW:
> You're full of it. Get out of the light—I'm comb-
> ing my hair.
> O.K., what's destiny? (*Combing her hair.*)

THE KID:
> It's doing what you want to do. Destiny is only
> a word but it's turned into a religion. Then it's
> laughed at.

HARLOW:
> Why not?

THE KID:
> It should be.

HARLOW:
> WHAT MATTERS?

THE KID:
> We're here!

HARLOW:
> Keep the fuck away from me!

THE KID:

I'm not even near.

HARLOW:

Before you can pry any secrets from me, you
must first find the real me! Which one will you
pursue?

THE KID:

You're right here!
—Sit on my lap . . .

HARLOW:

And touch your thing?

THE KID:

There's nobody here!

HARLOW:

Just like grownups, huh?
Why isn't blond hair on blue velvet enough?

THE KID:

Because you're a bag of meat!

HARLOW:

What do you mean you'd want ME?
Why isn't blond hair on blue velvet enough?
I'm a real blonde.

THE KID:

That's what I said!

HARLOW (*combing hair*):

You tore my panties up!

THE KID:

That's what I wanted.

HARLOW:

You're full of shit! If destiny is to tear a girl's panties up—then you're full of it!
Look at those poor rags.

THE KID:

Yeah.

HARLOW:

Look at 'em!

THE KID:

Sure.

HARLOW:

You tore my panties up!

THE KID:

Yeah!

HARLOW:

You tore them in half—and bit me on the toe
—and threw me on the floor—and ruined my stocking!

THE KID:

You ruined your stocking.

HARLOW:

You bit my fucking toe! AND TORE MY PAN-
TIES UP!

THE KID:

That's what you wanted!

HARLOW:

BULL SHIT!

75

THE KID:

That's what you said!
Before you can pry any secrets out of me, you must first find the real me! Which one will you pursue?

HARLOW:

Fuck off! (*Combs hair energetically.*)
That's a shitty destiny!

THE KID:

It's only a step.

HARLOW:

How can it be a step without being destiny?

THE KID:

Who knows?

HARLOW:

Yeah?

THE KID:

Yeah.

HARLOW:

You fucking rat! —I'm disheveled.

THE KID:

Good.

HARLOW:

I'm disheveled!

THE KID:

In eternity.
—You look good!

HARLOW:

Yeah, I'm disheveled in eternity—and that's destiny . . .

THE KID:

It doesn't matter! You're here and you look good!

HARLOW:

Where?

THE KID:

HERE! —And you look good!

HARLOW:

You said that and I'm tired of hearing it!

THE KID:

YOU LOOK GOOD!

HARLOW:

In eternity?

THE KID:

Yeah!

HARLOW:

Well, I don't like it!
—You're DUMB!

THE KID:

It doesn't matter!

HARLOW:

I'm sick of hearing you say it doesn't matter!

THE KID:

So what! We're here. It doesn't matter whether it matters—there's nobody around to watch!

HARLOW:

You're almost beautiful—you're so fucking dumb.

THE KID:

It doesn't matter!

HARLOW:

Awh shit!
There's nothing here but blond hair and blue velvet.

THE KID:

And a lot more.

HARLOW:

MORE WHAT?

THE KID:

It hasn't happened.— Sit on my lap.

HARLOW:

And lick your boots?

THE KID:

(No,) skip that.

HARLOW:

Skip it, huh?

THE KID:

Yeah, skip it. Sit on my lap.

HARLOW:

You're a maniac! What if I don't? What'll you do—tear my dress up?— Or kick my head?

THE KID:

I might.

78

HARLOW:

You might, huh?
YOU WOULDN'T DARE!

THE KID:

That's what you said before.

HARLOW:

O.K., I said it before.

THE KID:

What?

HARLOW:

Whatever I said.— Whatever I said, I said before.

THE KID:

That's right. (yeah)

HARLOW:

You monomaniac! You're so fucking dumb you
make me puke! You're so screwed up you might
do anything.

THE KID:

That's right.

HARLOW:

YOU'RE DUMB!

THE KID:

You're beautiful!

HARLOW:

YOU'RE DUMB! DUMB! DUMB!

THE KID:

Does it matter?

HARLOW (*pause*):
I DON'T KNOW.

THE KID:
Don't know what?

HARLOW:
Does it matter?

THE KID:
Yeah.

HARLOW:
You said nothing MATTERS!

THE KID:
It matters to ME.

(*Pause.*)

HARLOW:
Why don't you want me to lick your boots?

THE KID:
I changed my mind!

HARLOW:
In eternity?

THE KID:
Sit on my lap.

HARLOW:
And lick your boots?

THE KID:
We're divine and we're flesh and blood and
anything else is shit! IF WE DON'T DO WHAT
WE WANT—WE'RE NOT DIVINE! What **do**
you want?

HARLOW:

I don't know.

—You dumb cunt!

(*Looking.*) Where are my shoes?

THE KID:

I'll put them on your feet.

HARLOW:

The fuck you will!

Get out of my way.

THE KID:

Where would you go?

HARLOW:

I'll stay right here.

THE KID:

In eternity?

HARLOW:

Yeah. (*Finds shoes.*)

THE KID:

Is that what you want?

HARLOW:

Yeah, I'm going to stay right here!

THE KID:

There's nobody here to watch!

HARLOW: (*starts to put on shoe.*)

THE KID:

Don't put them on!

HARLOW:

Why not!

81

THE KID:

We're divine, Babe, divine!

HARLOW:

Maybe I won't—I like the look on your face.
I like to see you be a cunt! (*Stretches her legs
out—arching her feet.*)

THE KID:

What do you want?

HARLOW (*mocking*):

Well, what do you want?— Or maybe I shouldn't
ask—I already know!

THE KID:

How do you know?

HARLOW:

I heard what you say. You said it over and over
till it makes me puke!
—Where's my comb?

THE KID:

Look yourself!
It's on the table under your shoes.

HARLOW:

I know that—I just like to hear you talk!

THE KID:

Yeah!
What do you want?

HARLOW:

What if I said—"whatever you want"?

THE KID:

You're full of shit!

HARLOW:

GOD DAMN YOU, I'M SICK OF THIS!

THE KID:

Shut up, and sit on my lap!

HARLOW:

What does it matter if I do or don't?

THE KID:

It matters in eternity!

HARLOW:

Like being a bag of meat matters?

THE KID:

Yeah.

HARLOW:

What are we doing here?

THE KID:

It matters but I don't give a shit!

HARLOW:

You mean we're HERE!

THE KID:

Yeah.

HARLOW:

What'll we do?

THE KID:

WHAT I WANT!

HARLOW:

WHAT ABOUT ME?

THE KID:

Whatever you want!

HARLOW:

Yeah!
You're a dumb fuck!

THE KID:

And you're a bag of meat!

HARLOW:

And nothing more?

THE KID:

Where we are—only the bag of meat matters.

HARLOW:

Because there's nobody around to watch?

THE KID:

Yeah.

HARLOW:

And you tore my panties up.

THE KID:
Yes.

HARLOW:

And you bit me on the toe!

THE KID:

Yeah.

HARLOW:

And you threw me down on the floor!

THE KID:

Yeah.

HARLOW:

And you might do anything you want!

THE KID:
Sure.

HARLOW:
And what about me?

THE KID:
That's up to you.

HARLOW:
What if I sit on your lap?

THE KID:
You called me a cunt!

HARLOW:
YEAH, WITH YOUR HAIR HANGING DOWN
TO YOUR ASS AND BUCK TEETH!

THE KID:
What does it matter?

HARLOW:
IT MATTERS PLENTY, YOU FUCKING SHIT!
(*In fury.*) WHAT IF I SIT ON YOUR LAP!

THE KID:
Try it and see!

HARLOW:
I wouldn't touch you with a dirty stick!
(*Pause.*)
What if I did sit on your lap?

THE KID:
Try it and see.

HARLOW:
DON'T GET NEAR ME!!

85

THE KID:

I didn't move.

HARLOW:

You're full of it, buddy!
Look at my pants!
(*Holding them up.*)

THE KID:

So what!

HARLOW:

Stay right where you are!

THE KID:

Shut up! (*Not moving.*)

HARLOW:

What do you want?

THE KID:

Whatever I say I want!

HARLOW:

You said you wanted me to lick your boots!

THE KID:

O.K., do what you want.

HARLOW:

And now you don't.

THE KID:

Sit on my lap!

HARLOW:

WHAT IF I WALK OVER AND SIT ON YOUR
LAP?

THE KID:
Yeah.

HARLOW:
What if I do?

THE KID:
Try it and see.

HARLOW:
What would you do?

THE KID:
How would I know?
—Can't you guess?

HARLOW:
What do you want me to do?

THE KID:
I already said.

HARLOW:
Rub your joint?

THE KID:
Yeah. That's a place to start.

HARLOW (*hurls panties at him*):
THERE'S A START!

THE KID:
—We're already HERE. We don't need a start.

HARLOW:
Yeah, that's what YOU said!

THE KID:
We've started.

HARLOW:

Oh yeah! Fuck you!

THE KID:

What do you want?

HARLOW:

To look at the walls. (*She walks stroking the walls.*)

(THE KID *takes out handkerchief and polishes toes of his boots.*)

HARLOW:

WHAT IF I SAID YOU'RE NOT A CUNT?

THE KID:

So what! (*Polishing.*)

HARLOW:

WHAT IF I SAID YOU'RE NOT A CUNT?

THE KID:

So what!

HARLOW:

I've got to use words!

THE KID:

Oh yeah!

HARLOW:

WHAT DO YOU WANT? What the goddamn Hell do you want?

THE KID:

I want whatever I want!

HARLOW:

I've got to use words!

THE KID:
   Oh yeah!

HARLOW:
   I like you. (*Suddenly*:)
   You're insane and violent but I like you!

THE KID:
   So what!

HARLOW:
   I've got to use words!

THE KID:
   Oh yeah!

HARLOW:
   What do you want.

THE KID:
   I want whatever I want!

HARLOW:
   Well?

THE KID:
   Whatever I want!

HARLOW:
   Well WHAT do you want?

THE KID:
   Maybe I want to be beautiful!

HARLOW:
   Awh! WHAT DO YOU WANT?

THE KID:
   Before you can pry any secrets from me, you
   must first find the real me! Which one will you
   pursue?

89

HARLOW:

What makes you think I want to pry secrets from YOU?

THE KID:

Because I'm so beautiful.

HARLOW:

So what!

THE KID:

You want to be as beautiful as I am.

HARLOW:

Oh yeah!

THE KID:

Before you can pry any secrets from me, you must first find the real me! Which one will you pursue?

HARLOW (*coming closer*):

What makes you think I want to pry any secrets from you?

THE KID:

Because I'm so beautiful.

HARLOW:

So what!

THE KID:

You want to be as beautiful as I am!

HARLOW:

Oh yeah! (*Kneels quickly and grabs his boots.*)
I'VE GOT YOU!
YOU'RE BEAUTIFUL!

THE KID:

It's an illusion!

(HARLOW *hugs the boots and caresses them.*)

HARLOW:

There are rainbows on them—rainbows reflected on sheer black!

(KID *reaches over and takes Harlow's head.*)

THE KID:

Now I've got your blond hair in my hands.

HARLOW:

There are rainbows on them—rainbows reflected on sheer black!

THE KID:

Now I've got your blond hair in my hands!

HARLOW:

There are rainbows on them—rainbows reflected on sheer black!

THE KID:

Now I've got your blond hair in my hands.

HARLOW (*looking up at* KID):

You've got my blond hair in your hands.
There's nobody around to watch!
You tore my panties up and you bit my toe!

THE KID:

Yeah.

HARLOW:

There's nobody around to watch.

91

THE KID:
No, there's not.

HARLOW:
What'll we do?

(THE KID *pulls* HARLOW *up into his lap.*)

THE KID (*looking into Harlow's eyes*):
—Now I've got your blond hair in my hands.

HARLOW:
—And we're all alone!

(HARLOW *sitting on Kid's lap with one arm around his neck—he kisses her on the shoulder and neck —she strokes his cock . . .*)

HARLOW:
My God, we're really here!

(*They begin to twist in the chair—*THE KID *slips gradually to the floor at Harlow's feet.*)

HARLOW:
And we're all alone!

(*Kneeling,* THE KID *takes Harlow's foot in his hands and kisses it. He kisses the other foot. He presses his head against her thighs and holds it there. His hands clutch her bare feet behind his back. He lets loose of her feet pressing his head more tightly against her thighs. She arches her back. He grasps her feet again burying his head in her thighs. He raises his head as if to speak and drops it to her thighs again. He lets loose of her feet and grasps them again. He lets loose of her feet and reaches up and moves her dress up her*

92

thighs. He clutches her feet behind him again. He grasps her thighs and presses his face between them, kissing her. HARLOW *stiffens and arches her body . . .)*

HARLOW (*ecstatically*):
STAR! STAR! STAR! OH MY GOD—! STAR!
STAR! STAR! STAR! STAR! OH MY GOD—!
STAR! STAR! YOU'RE NEXT! OH MY GOD—!
BLUE-BLACK STAR! STAR! STAR! STAR!
STAR! STAR! STAR! STAR! STAR! STAR!
STAR! STAR! STAR! STAR! STAR! STAR!
STAR! STAR!

AFTERWORD

The Beard was presented four times before direct police intervention. First by the Actor's Workshop of San Francisco, where it proved to be too much for that organization. Despite the efforts of the director, the author and the actors, the Workshop establishment impeded in every possible way a performance of the play—including forbidding the presence of newspaper reviewers. Despite this censorship, Michael Grieg's review (heralding the play as the "most effectively upsetting and creatively stimulating work by a local writer that the workshop has ever presented") slipped into the San Francisco *Chronicle*. *The Beard* was next presented at the huge rock and roll *Fillmore Auditorium* to a wildly enthusiastic capacity crowd, where it was accompanied by Anthony Martin's light projections and a sound system utilizing rock music. The third and fourth performances of Michael McClure's *The Beard* took place at San Francisco's North Beach theater night club, *The Committee*. These two performances were surreptitiously tape-recorded by the San Francisco Police Department, and at the fifth presentation, again at *The Committee*, police interrupted the ending of the play by filming it with whirring cameras, and then hurried backstage to arrest Mr. Bright (*Billy the Kid*) and Miss Dixon (*Harlow*). Alternately, the actors were charged with "obscenity," then "conspiracy to commit a felony," and finally with "lewd and dissolute conduct in a public place."

Twelve days later, *The Beard,* now represented by the American Civil Liberties Union (after an offer of help from Melvin Belli), was presented in Berkeley by Rare Angel Productions to a capacity crowd, which included more than one hundred expert witnesses. These witnesses, invited by Rare Angel Productions, included Lawrence Ferlinghetti, Alan Watts, members of the academic community, members of the clergy, and photographers and tape-recording crews whose function was to record the police filming and taping of the performance. Seven members of the Berkeley Police and District Attorney's department arrived two hours before the performance, and began harassment of the actors, the author, and the stage crew. Malcolm Burnstein of the ACLU and the author forbade any taping or filming of the performance, a directive ignored by the police and D.A.'s office. The evening turned into a "happening," with the audience wildly cheering and applauding the attorneys, the author, the actors, and denouncing the civil authorities. After the performance there were speeches by invited celebrities, and the police left quietly. It was not until five days later that Berkeley also brought charges of "lewd and dissolute conduct in a public place."

After five months of litigation, Marshall Krause, of the ACLU, persuaded the San Francisco Superior Court that the charges were inappropriate, and the case was dropped from court—an important legal precedent having been set. Following the San Francisco court action, the Berkeley court withdrew its charges. Rare Angel Productions, now free to perform *The Beard* in California, is resuming its production of the play.

VKTMS

Orestes in Scenes

*The behavior and spirit
of inner violence*

Gray hungers fledged with desire of transgression, salt-slimed beaks, from the sharp
rock shores of the world and the secret waters . . .   Robinson Jeffers

CAST

ORESTES—son of Clytemnestra and Agamemnon.

ELEKTRA—Orestes' sister.

PYLADES—friend of Orestes.

HELEN—Helen of Troy, wife of Orestes' uncle Menelaos.

NOSTRINA—slave of Helen and then slave of Elektra.

THYRSOS—slave of Helen and then slave of Orestes.

BASILOS—slave of Helen and then slave of Pylades.

Orestes and his sister Elektra go with Pylades to kill their mother Clytemnestra and her lover their Uncle Aegisthos. They do so to avenge Clytemnestra's murder of their father Agamemnon.

Orestes and Elektra ask their father's brother Menelaos to defend them at their murder trial while they are in sanctuary.

Angered that Menelaos will not speak for them, Orestes, Elektra, and Pylades leave sanctuary and kill Menelaos' wife Helen and her daughter Hermione and their slaves.

After the murder, Orestes, Elektra, and Pylades are metamorphosed into war chariots. Helen is metamorphosed into a star.

The play begins.

They remember.

The play opens in blackness and silence.
Then voices are heard making cricket frog calls in acous-
tic clusters. The frogs are people's voices and not on
tape. They say: I-you-me-rose-pink-black-light . . . I-
you-me-rose-pink-black-light . . . I-you-me-rose-pink-
black-light . . .
Next the songs of wild dogs are heard in the near dis-
tance—clusters of singing barks and pleasant yelps. The
wild dog voices are also human voices and not on tape.
(At points in the play the wild dog and frog voices are
used as background or punctuation but not in black-
outs.)
Light comes up a bit on the stage. There are fine tendrils
of smoke or mist. It is not unpleasant or dracula-esque.
The stage floor is gray carpet.
The lights come up more. Then more.
Upstage are three two-wheeled war chariots of ivory,
burnished steel and gold. The chariots have large fea-
tureless masks on their tailgates. The tailgates face the
audience. Set in the blank masks are live faces with real
arms beneath. The faces are ORESTES, ELEKTRA, *and*
PYLADES. *The three are young and good-looking.* ORES-
TES *and* PYLADES *have craggy features and long hair*
and they hold bloody two-edged swords. Their arms are
bloody. ELEKTRA *holds flowers. They have their eyes*
closed.
HELEN *is dimly seen. She is seated on a gold throne on a*
high platform at upstage right. She is in darkness, look-
ing, with closed eyes, into the distance. HELEN *is blonde,*
naked, and wears high platform sandals.
Downstage three slaves lounge in a tableau. They are
dressed in high heels, gray short tunics with blousy,
sleeveless tops, and belts of rolled cloth.
BASILOS, *the slave who will serve* PYLADES, *is an agile*

old man with a white beard. There's a bloody white bandage wrapped around his head in turban style.

NOSTRINA *is attractive. She has an arm hacked off and she is frozen in tableau trying to close it with a tourniquet. She serves* ELEKTRA.

THYRSOS *is thirty. A large raw belly wound is seen through his torn blouse. He serves* ORESTES.

The play moves slowly and deliberately—and as if it were an organism in shock. The blackouts separate the scenes sharply like bubbles.

> (BASILOS, *the white-bearded slave, moves and squats on his hunkers. He bends over and then shakes and throws huge dice onto the gray carpet.*)

BASILOS (*reading dice*):
Seven. (*Pause. Throws. Reads.*) Seven. (*Throws again.*) Seven. (*Throws.*) Seven. (*Throws.*) Seven. (*Throws.*) Seven. (*Throws.*) Seven. (*Throws.*) Seven. (*Throws.*) SEVEN!

THYRSOS (*cattily, without looking at dice*):
I don't believe it!

BASILOS (*throwing thoughtfully*):
Three! (*Throws.*) Three! (*Throws.*) Three! (*Throws. Pauses. Looks slowly at* THYRSOS.)

THYRSOS:
Let me guess, dear. (*Slight pause.*) Three?

> (NOSTRINA *is working at her wound trying to tie a cord around the stump of her arm within the blouse.*)

NOSTRINA (*in a small desperate voice*):
Help me!

THYRSOS:

Bitch! If we were going to die, we'd be dead by now.

NOSTRINA (*succeeding with tourniquet*):

There, I stopped the blood again.

(*BLACKOUT. Blackouts are about eight seconds duration.*)

* * *

(*LIGHTS UP. Scene as before.* BASILOS *is slowly throwing dice and contemplating them.* THYRSOS *is looking away and not watching.*)

NOSTRINA (*looking around, tightening tourniquet*):

I never thought it would be like this.

THYRSOS (*snickers*):

It is.

(BASILOS *continues throwing dice.*)

THYRSOS:

Threes?

(*Small pause.*)

BASILOS:

Yes.

THYRSOS (*listening, indicating with head*):

What are those?

BASILOS (*listens*):

Wild dogs. Crickets.

(*BLACKOUT.*)

106

*　*　*

(*LIGHTS UP. Scene as before.*)

THYRSOS (*rubbing his legs with hand*):
I wonder if I'll be able to shave?

NOSTRINA (*pointing to* ORESTES):
When Orestes chopped off my arm he shouted:
THIS IS FOR MY SISTER ELEKTRA!

BASILOS:
So you'll be her servant.

NOSTRINA (*puzzled*):
Me?

THYRSOS:
Yes.

BASILOS:
And Pylades cracked my head open—so I work for him.

THYRSOS:
And Orestes put his chopper through my tummy.
I'll have to pull him around.

NOSTRINA:
That's the way it is?

BASILOS:
Yes. Once a slave always a slave.

THYRSOS:
We get to change masters.

(*BLACKOUT.*)

* * *

(*LIGHTS UP. Scene as before*.)

NOSTRINA (*recalling the shock*):
It was revolting. They chopped Helen up.

THYRSOS:
She's a cunt. The worst master I ever had.

BASILOS:
You haven't had that many.

THYRSOS:
She's a barbarian. A Greek. The Greeks don't think
we're human. Pylades shouted: "DEATH TO
HELEN—THE CAUSE OF THE WAR! AND
HER EFFEMINATE SLAVES!"
Us!
Have you noticed it's hard to think?

BASILOS:
It's shock.

THYRSOS:
Will we get over it?

BASILOS:
There doesn't seem to be any time.

THYRSOS:
Meaning what?

BASILOS:
I don't know.

NOSTRINA:
What happened to us?

(*Points to* PYLADES, ORESTES, ELEKTRA.) What happened to them?

BASILOS:
   I don't know.

NOSTRINA:
   Why not?

BASILOS (*numbly*):
   The shock.

THYRSOS:
   You don't know anything!

   (*BLACKOUT.*)

* * *

   (*LIGHTS UP. Scene as before.*)

THYRSOS (*looking at* ORESTES, ELEKTRA, & PYLADES):
   They were human . . . but they turned to war chariots or whatever those are. (*Remembering.*) They broke into the palace in battle armor. I was shaving my legs. Basilos was throwing dice and Nostrina was butchering a hen.

NOSTRINA (*remembering*):
   Helen was in the pool.

BASILOS:
   That's it. Helen was asking about the shouting and clanging. She sent Hermione to the roof to see who was fighting.

109

NOSTRINA (*slowly*):

And then Orestes and Elektra and Pylades broke in. Nobody knew the fight was that close. Or who it was.

THYRSOS (*not fast*):

Helen climbed out of the pool naked and started screaming.

NOSTRINA:

We fell down around their feet and started supplicating them. Thyrsos, you were great.

THYRSOS:

I'm not bad at that—supplicating and writhing are my specialty.

BASILOS:

The trial was going on and Orestes and Elektra were being judged for murdering their mother Clytemnestra and their uncle Aegisthos. They were in the sanctuary on the hill but they left and fought their way to the palace.

THYRSOS:

That's it.

BASILOS:

Hard to get it straight.

THYRSOS:

Shock! Look at my gut! No wonder I can't think.

BASILOS:

They knew they were condemned to death. So they fought their way here.

NOSTRINA:

Fought their way here to kill their aunt Helen. It doesn't make sense.

THYRSOS:

Pylades had a lot to do with it. They were blood crazy. Who knows what it meant to them. Who knows what they thought they were doing.
It's going to go black. (*Looks around*.)
It's like a pulse.

BASILOS:

Yes.

(*BLACKOUT*.)

*   *   *

(*LIGHTS UP. Scene as before*.)

THYRSOS (*reconstructing*):

First they killed Clytemnestra and Aegisthos and afterwards while they were being tried for murder fought their way from the sanctuary and broke in and killed us and Helen.

NOSTRINA:

And Hermione.

THYRSOS:

Then there was a metamorphosis. They metamorphosed into war carts. Now we're here. Wherever that is.

BASILOS:

In shock.

THYRSOS:

It's not that bad.

NOSTRINA:

No, it's not.

111

(BLACKOUT.)

* * *

(LIGHTS UP. Scene as before.)

BASILOS *(throwing dice)*:
Three . . . *(Throws.)* Four . . . *(Throws.)* Three . . .
(Throws.) Four . . . *(Throws.)* Three.

*(ORESTES speaks without opening his eyes. THE
SLAVES stop moving and then freeze.)*

ORESTES *(sniffing)*
Smell that! It's shit. I can smell shit.

PYLADES *(pause, without opening his eyes)*:
Yes. it's shit.

ELEKTRA *(with eyes still closed)*:
Are there flowers here?

ORESTES:
You're not here, Elektra.

PYLADES:
We're in a field.

ORESTES:
Yes, that's it.

ELEKTRA:
But we were in Argos. We broke into the palace and
you and Pylades killed Helen.

ORESTES:
Yes.

ELEKTRA:
> Then I'm here. It's Argos. This is Argos. It's a city not a field.

ORESTES:
> Yes.

BASILOS (*goes back to throwing dice*):
> Three . . . Four . . . Three . . . Four . . .

ELEKTRA:
> Why are we like this?

PYLADES:
> I don't like it.

BASILOS (*throwing dice*):
> Three. . . Four. . . Three. . . Four. . . Seven. . . Seven. . .

ORESTES (*realizing it*):
> It's metamorphosis!

PYLADES:
> WE WERE CHANGED INTO WAR CARTS!
> (*BLACKOUT.*)

* * *

(*LIGHTS UP. Scene as before.*)

ELEKTRA (*eyes still closed*):
> This is Argos.

ORESTES:
> How old are we?

ELEKTRA:

I'm three.

PYLADES:

I'm not here.

ORESTES:

No. You're in Uncle Menelaos' city Sparta. You're growing up. Elektra and I are in Argos. She's three, I'm almost four.

(NOSTRINA *and* THYRSOS *take the harness shafts of the chariots and move them so that* ORESTES *and* ELEKTRA *face each other. At appropriate moments* NOSTRINA *and* THYRSOS *push* ORESTES *and* ELEKTRA *towards each other—or draw them back from one another. The movements make a rhapsodic childish rhythm.* ORESTES *and* ELEKTRA *speak like children.*)

ELEKTRA (*opening eyes widely*):

This is play wine. (*Holding up imaginary cup with both hands.*) We're drinking!

ORESTES (*opening eyes, holding up imaginary cup, speaks as a child*):

This is wine!

ELEKTRA:

Daddy is back from the war! "Hurray Agamemnon!" they're shouting.

ORESTES:

He killed the city of Troy.

ELEKTRA:

They brought Aunt Helen back. Isn't that right, Orestes?

114

ORESTES:

Yes, that's right. And also slaves, and furs, and money and gold. Mommy is giving Daddy a bath. When he's clean we'll sit by him in the big room.

ELEKTRA:

Drink more play wine. (*Pours imaginary wine.*)

ORESTES:

First you must give some to the black gods. (*He spits imaginary wine onto floor.*)

ELEKTRA:

No. No. You don't spit it, you pour it. Daddy must be very clean now. It's a long time.
Can you feel time?

ORESTES:

No, I'm a man. I feel war.

ELEKTRA (*proudly*):

We're waiting for Papa.

(ORESTES *pauses—listens.*)

ORESTES:

Listen!

(ORESTES *and* ELEKTRA *listen.*)

ELEKTRA:

Mama screamed. That's Mama!

(*They listen.*)

ORESTES:

Papa's yelling. He's screaming. I'm scared.

(*They listen.*)

ELEKTRA:

Mama's yelling and laughing. Uncle Aegisthos is yelling and laughing—it makes echoes.

(*Pause*.)

ORESTES:

I think Papa is dead.

ELEKTRA (*frightened, changing subject as a child does*):

What should we do about the wine?

(*BLACKOUT*.)

* * *

(*LIGHTS UP*. ORESTES, PYLADES, ELEKTRA *are facing upstage. Downstage* NOSTRINA *is standing.* THYRSOS *and* BASILOS *are sitting looking up at her.* BASILOS *is combing his beard with his fingers*.)

NOSTRINA (*with satisfaction*):

I remember better now: I was dying.

THYRSOS (*can't stand reference to death*):

Don't say that! Don't say *dying*!

NOSTRINA:

You were already killed. Orestes killed you first. It looked fast. Then he chased Menthia and she ran out the window into the court. She's safe.

THYRSOS (*bored, dislikes Menthia*):

Who cares?

NOSTRINA:

Then Pylades chopped open Basilos' head with one big hit.

116

BASILOS:

Yes, that's right. His eyes were bloodshot, they were red and they looked like they were square. They were both squinted and held wide open. They looked like a boar hog's eyes. His face was in pads of muscle and stripes of skin held rigid. . . . He ran as hard as he could at me and he swung it. I felt like my head exploded before he hit me. I didn't feel a thing.

THYRSOS:

Was he still yelling?

BASILOS:

Yes. I think so.

NOSTRINA:

Orestes had come back in. Menthia got away.

THYRSOS:

I hope the bitch doesn't find my razor!

NOSTRINA:

And Orestes ran at me, I remember the stubby muscular legs. I was looking up at them and he stopped. Suddenly. I saw the sword go up. High. And he yelled that this was for Elektra.

THYRSOS:

He wanted to make you her servant.

NOSTRINA:

When it hit, it spun me around. Half way. Like the roof fell in. I didn't believe it. My arm was lying there. I was holding the blood in with my hand. Squeezing my arm. Everything had silver light and was gigantic. Orestes went back and hit Helen. She fell down—naked—blonde hair—spout of blood.

117

THYRSOS (*repulsed*):
Yuhh!

NOSTRINA:
Then Pylades hit her. I could just see the big blur of
it. Then Pylades hit her again. Then Orestes hit her.
They were chopping her over and over knocking
pieces off. They didn't say anything. They were
making loud breath sounds and noise in their
throats. I had the impression Elektra was singing,
but I don't know. Hermione came in screaming,
flying at them. Tears all over her face. Orestes hit
Hermione with his fist and she fell down flat. The
three of them stuffed her in the big basket and shut
it and threw it into the pool. Maybe I heard bubbles. A drowning scream.
Then I . . .
(*Looks around*.) There's going to be blackness.

(*BLACKOUT.*)

* * *

(*LIGHTS UP.* ELEKTRA *stage right,* ORESTES *center,*
PYLADES *stage left, are in a row facing the audience.* NOSTRINA, THYRSOS, BASILOS *are behind
them holding the chariot shafts. They move the pro-
tagonists forward and back when appropriate*.)

ELEKTRA:
We're like starfish on the piles. The yellow ones.
The slow ones.

ORESTES:
How long will this be? I don't like it like this!

PYLADES:

It's a metamorphosis. Your great-grandfather Pelops was served to the gods by his father Tantalos. But Demeter brought him back to life. Everything's changing.

ELEKTRA:

They don't have any eyes or brains. They're aware, but only of big things like waves beating against them—or being dry above the waterline when the tide drops. They're conscious, but not of much.
(*Pause*.)
There's less happening now.

ORESTES (*to* PYLADES):

You drowned Hermione! That's what made this happen.

PYLADES (*swung by* BASILOS *to face* ORESTES):

The Hell you say!

ORESTES:

You caused this to happen! It was killing Helen's daughter Hermione that brought on the overload and made the metamorphosis. A god was watching. Saw that it was too much and caused us to change. I know that we were changed just as she died. Now, look, we're no better than dead and nothing. I expected to die but I didn't know what was coming.

PYLADES:

You hit her. In the forehead. She fell down.

ORESTES:

The idea was to hold her hostage. We could trade her. Bargain with her if she was alive. We could kill

119

Helen—avenge ourselves on Menelaos. Then hold her daughter Hermione hostage for our freedom.

PYLADES:

Or kill her if necessary—and then kill ourselves.

ORESTES:

But you had to go for Hermione. You're a fucking monster! There were pieces of my Aunt Helen all over the tiles. It smelled like shit! You had to push Hermione in the basket.

PYLADES:

Elektra dragged the basket over. She pulled it over to us.

ELEKTRA:

That's right. Yes. The basket was full of hen feathers—handfuls of brown feathers. I dragged it over to Hermione. My cousin was lying there. She didn't move. I started pushing her in the basket.

PYLADES:

That's the way it was.

ELEKTRA:

She's a little woman. She went in the basket easy. We all threw her in the pool.

ORESTES:

What caused this change?

PYLADES:

Helen. Helen caused it.

(*BLACKOUT.*)

* * *

(*LIGHTS UP on* HELEN *on her throne. Below* SLAVES *are lying on floor in darkness.*)

HELEN (*to herself, remembering*):

My name. Everyone's yelling my name. Nostrina is screaming. I'm out of the pool. The door crashes in. Pylades or Orestes reaches in. Somebody pulls the door bolt . . .

Menthia is running around shrieking.

I'm screaming. I'm screaming. I'm screaming.

Water is squirting out of my eyes and slobber out of my mouth.

I've never been so afraid.

I'm screaming.

Pylades is yelling!

Orestes has got blood red eyes!

Water is squirting out of my eyes and slobber out of my mouth.

I've never been so afraid.

He runs at me.

Nostrina is gasping.

(NOSTRINA *is on the floor below in darkness and gasping.*)

It's beyond fear. It's beyond pain. It's like I'm crazy.

It comes at me in pictures.

Picture of Thyrsos and blood all over him around the wound.

(THYRSOS, *on floor below in darkness, groans.*)

I'm screaming.

No sound. (*Listens.*)

Everything . . .

(*Listens.*)

Pylades walks deliberately to me. Soft on his feet.

(*BLACKOUT.*)

121

(*LIGHTS UP.* PYLADES, ORESTES, ELEKTRA *at front stage*—SLAVES *behind them holding shafts of chariots.*)

PYLADES:

Helen caused this. I know it! She's been changed into a star. God damn her! She's somewhere and she's a star. She's been changed all the way and she's a star. We've only been partly changed. We're chariots. War carts! We should have been heroes. Capital H Heroes and instead we're these. I can feel what happened. We should have continued through the metamorphosis but we're blocked!
We're stopped as *these*! I fucking hate it!
(*To* ORESTES *and* ELEKTRA.) Hey!

ELEKTRA (*eyes closed, voice like a child*):

This is Argos. I'm three. This is a long time ago or in the future. Mama lives with Uncle Aegisthos. They sleep in the big bed.

ORESTES:

I'm four and this is Argos.

(NOSTRINA *and* THYRSOS *take shafts of chariots and move them so that* ORESTES *and* ELEKTRA *face each other.* NOSTRINA *and* THYRSOS *draw them back and forth in a rhythm with the speech and actions.*)

ELEKTRA:

I'm happy that our Daddy Agamemnon is back from Troy. When he dies you can be king, Orestes. Orestes, I have wine in this vase. It's play wine. Here are cups. (*Holding imaginary two-handled cups and pouring wine into them.*) I add water to the wine. The water and the wine flow into each other and I don't spill any. We're drinking because Daddy is back.

ORESTES (*holding imaginary cup, raising it*):
This is wine. Pretty soon I will be king now. Daddy will make me king and then when I am king you will be the queen. I don't care if you're my sister, I'll make you the queen. You can be my sister and be the queen.

ELEKTRA:
What's going to happen to Uncle Aegisthos?

ORESTES:
I will kill him when I'm big. When I'm grown up.

ELEKTRA (*holding wine up*):
This is play wine. We're drinking. Is it right to kill Uncle Aegisthos?

ORESTES:
You have to kill people to be king.

ELEKTRA:
"Hurray Agamemnon!" they're shouting in the street. They're drinking and there's music. They're dancing.

ORESTES:
Father killed the city of Troy and he burned it down. He killed Paris and he brought Aunt Helen back to Uncle Menelaos. He brought back slaves with black hair and high heels and furs—and there are big gold shields. I saw one from the window. And there was cloth with orange flowers all over it.

ELEKTRA:

Mommy is giving Daddy a bath. That's what they always do when men come back. They're in the bedroom and when she gives him the bath he will be all clean and when he's clean we will go out to the big room and we'll sit by Daddy in the big room. He'll be shiny. He won't have any whiskers and his hair will be combed. He'll give us presents in the big room.

ORESTES:

When you drink you must give wine to the black gods—so they won't change things. (*He spits imaginary wine onto floor.*) There! (*He spits again.*) There!

ELEKTRA:

You don't spit it—you pour it.
(*She shows him.*)

ORESTES:

It's been a long time. I want to go to the big room.

ELEKTRA:

Can you feel time?

NOSTRINA (*looking around, then sitting still*):
There's a pulse. It's going black.

BASILOS:

Again?
Yes. Again.

ELEKTRA:

No.
It's O.K.
It's not going to.

(Lights dim down to HELEN.*)*

HELEN:

I am a star now and I am in space. Somewhere. And
it is O.K.
I am in space somewhere shining.

NOSTRINA (*Speaking of lights going to black*):
Yes it is.

(BLACKOUT.)

* * *

(LIGHTS UP. Scene as before.)

ORESTES (*as child*):

I feel war. I'm a man and men feel war. I can smell
it. I'll stand in ashes and smell the smoke—like the
smell on men's clothes when they come back.

ELEKTRA:

I don't like that.

ORESTES:

No.

PYLADES (*to no one*):

We are the fabric of nature which is like cloth—a
cloth rolled up. And if Helen is a star then our pattern is to be war carts.
We are rigid. It is hard to think.

ELEKTRA (*proudly*):

We're waiting for Papa, Mama is bathing him.

(ORESTES and ELEKTRA listen.)

125

ORESTES:
Listen! That's Mother.

ELEKTRA (*listens*):
Mama screamed! Listen, Mama's screaming.
Hear Mama!
What's happening Orestes?

(*Pause.* ORESTES *and* ELEKTRA *listen.*)

ELEKTRA:
Mama is laughing. Loud. She's laughing. I don't hear Father. That's Uncle Aegisthos. He's yelling and laughing—Uncle Aegisthos is yelling and laughing and it makes echoes.

(*Pause.*)

ORESTES:
I think Papa is dead, Elektra.

PYLADES (*as if in a trance*):
The fabric of nature is a rolled up cloth—NO!—it is wadded! It is all wound together. Every surface touches another and only a clean gesture drives us through it . . . Only a clean strike that slices the flesh. But we killed Helen cleanly with anger and ferocity. Being bold for vengeance is clean!

ELEKTRA (*quietly*):
This is play wine.

ORESTES (*turning head as if looking*):
Now we're somewhere else. Elektra, we're not here anymore.

HELEN (*to herself*):
I am in the sky and my light comes from me—and

126

the light is there. But I am many places. There is more light there than here.

PYLADES:

What we are is rigid. We're armor. We can't think clear because we have become facts. We are only ourselves. We have no penetration.

ELEKTRA:

I only know what I am saying. There isn't any past or future or now. Just what I say is what I know.

ORESTES:

We've got to kill them, Elektra, or we have no honor.

ELEKTRA:

Grandpa Tyndareos says you're kill-crazy, Orestes.

ORESTES:

He's not our grandpa. Grandpa was a giant white swan.

(BASILOS *is dicing. He calls the numbers quietly—* Seven — Nine — Nine — Nine — Seven — Nine — Nine—Nine—Seven—*while* NOSTRINA *and* THYR- SOS *watch from their places at the shafts of* ORES- TES *and* ELEKTRA.)

ELEKTRA:

But she's our mother. We can't kill our mother.

ORESTES:

She's evil.

ELEKTRA:

Yes, she's evil.

127

ORESTES:
She killed our father. We heard it.

ELEKTRA:
We were children.

ORESTES:
We heard it.

ELEKTRA:
Aegisthos killed him.

ORESTES:
No, she killed him. We know it.

ELEKTRA:
She hated him because he killed our sister Iphigenia. I was there in Aulis. I saw it. I was a baby. I was there.

ORESTES:
No matter. It doesn't matter.

ELEKTRA:
Just kill Aegisthos—don't kill our mother.

PYLADES:
They both have to die. Reason says kill both of them. You hate them, don't you?

ELEKTRA (*to herself*):
I hate them. But she's my mother—and he's my uncle.
I want to do what is right.
I want to disappear.
I want to be nothing.
I want to disappear in the fields. I look at the yellow flowers and the rocks and the places where the earth

cracks open in patterns and one can see the mois-
ture and I want to go into the cracks. I want to do
what is right and I'd be happy that way.
There's no reason to kill.
You know, I only know what I'm saying.
That's all. I only know what I'm saying.

PYLADES:

All we are is what we're saying unless we do something. I'll help you. I can help you.

ELEKTRA:

Why do you want to help me?

PYLADES:

Because I love you.

ORESTES:

I've given you to Pylades—to marry—if we live
after this.

ELEKTRA (*disbelief with edge of revulsion*):
Me?

(*BLACKOUT.*)

* * *

(*LIGHTS UP on* HELEN *above and on* NOSTRINA
below.)

HELEN:

Pylades walks deliberately to me. He's smiling and
he raises his sword up and to the side. Then swings
it back. It's a picture.

NOSTRINA (*facing away from* HELEN):
>It was Orestes who hit you first. He ran at you yell-
>ing. Kill-crazy. Blood was squirting out of me. Men-
>thia was screaming.

HELEN:
>I remember.
>Every piece of me knows.
>My light is pieces and rays and that's what I am.
>I am here in light.

NOSTRINA (*to herself*):
>Everything was silver then.

HELEN:
>Everything is silver.

NOSTRINA:
>There was a change.

HELEN:
>There is a metamorphosis.
>They are both swinging at me.
>Pieces of me go everywhere.
>Everything becomes one instant.
>Everything becomes one instant for everyone as
>Hermione drowns.
>The light begins then. It is here but also every-
>where else.

>(*Lights up on* ELEKTRA.)

ELEKTRA:
>Elektra? Why me Elektra?

PYLADES:
>Because I love you. I love your brother.

ORESTES:

I give you to Pylades because you are my sister and he's my friend. He'll help us do what we've got to do. We must kill Aegisthos and Clytemnestra.

ELEKTRA:

Listen Orestes, I want to do what's right. But killing our mother isn't it.

ORESTES:

To kill those who dishonor you is right. To end those who murder your father is right.

ELEKTRA:

She's our parent.

ORESTES:

We kill for the honor of our bloodline. We're part gods. I come back and they have taken my kingdom. They sent me away to die. I was a child. I came back to you in Argos with Pylades. Ask Pylades. He says it is true—that to kill a murderer of your father is as sweet as it is to walk by a pond in the hills.

ELEKTRA:

But we'll die. They'll kill us. They'll say we are abominable. They say Pylades loves to kill and that you listened to him. They'll execute us. We couldn't get away. If we escaped, where could we go? We don't have anything.

ORESTES:

This is not something you can weigh.

PYLADES:

Right. The truth crushes, but it's truth.

(*BLACKOUT.*)

131

* * *

(LIGHTS UP. ORESTES, ELEKTRA, PYLADES *at rest with eyes closed.* SLAVES *in a group—downstage center.)*

THYRSOS *(noncommittal)*:
So.

BASILOS:
So.

THYRSOS:
Can you think better?

BASILOS:
No. No. I don't think so. Maybe it's clearer.
There are some moments.

THYRSOS *(noncommittal)*:
Then you can see it.

BASILOS:
I can see all right.
When I see, I can see it.

THYRSOS:
There's no pain. There could be. I wouldn't like
that. But maybe this *is* pain. Maybe this is all there
is to pain. If we knew what is going on, it might be
enormously painful. We might hurt all the time if
we knew everything. I don't like discomfort. I like
pleasure. This is better than being in agony. If I had
my body this would hurt.

BASILOS:
What do you think you're wearing? What you've got
on is *you*. There's no more or less of it than that.

PYLADES (*to* BASILOS):

Swing me around. (BASILOS *swings* PYLADES *slowly.*)
The truth crushes.
What Aegisthos said to Clytemnestra was horrible.

ELEKTRA:

You don't know what he said!

PYLADES:

He said, "Agamemnon's coming back.
He has one ship . . . and more behind him.
I'm afraid.
Agamemnon will kill me. And you.
He'll kill you for loving me."

ORESTES:

Listen, Elektra.

PYLADES:

He said, "I am afraid, Clytemnestra.
Everyone will kill me if I kill him.
He had the priest kill your baby Iphigenia."

ELEKTRA:

I saw the priest. I was an infant, too, but I saw it.
The priest cut her throat like she was a baby sheep
and everyone yelled. They liked it.

ORESTES:

Then mother said . . .

ELEKTRA:

You can't know this!

ORESTES:

She said, "You kill him Aegisthos.
I'll say I did it in rage."

133

He said, "You've got to do it and you've got to feel
rage.
It doesn't matter that everything is passed and dif-
ferent now.
It is not different to him.
He's a butcher coming to get both of us when he
learns.
Or, we could end it now.
You and I could run off the cliff."

ELEKTRA (*to* NOSTRINA):
Swing me around! (*Towards* PYLADES.) I don't want
to hear this!

ORESTES:
You can hear it as clearly as I can—and it was worse
than that. We both know it was rottener than that.
It was sweaty and clammy. It became cold-blooded
and then they laughed about it and they got drunk.
And then it got really good. They made jokes.

ELEKTRA:
No!

ORESTES:
Yes.

ELEKTRA (*thinking*):
You're right.

ORESTES:
Then our mother put on a face of absolute hypocrisy
and went out to meet him.

ELEKTRA:
Pylades, why don't we make love better?

PYLADES:

Because there is so little time.

ELEKTRA:

Why is there so little?

PYLADES:

Because so much fills it. It must be simplified. Everything is too complex. We must strike through it.

ORESTES:

Only if we kill Aegisthos and mother will we let loose the god blood to flow around in us. Our first ancestor Tantalos was a son of Zeus. The god blood should only be inside of bodies that are worth being the holder of it. But not mother. Not her body.

PYLADES:

That's right. And there's more than that.

ELEKTRA:

Tantalos was not good. He stole his father Zeus' secrets.

PYLADES:

Right, but he was Tantalos.

When you stand between action and thinking you're like Tantalos. You can't get a drink in Hades because the water falls away beneath when you reach for it, and you can't stretch to the grapes because they raise up out of the reach of your fingers. Hades is real. It is all in the head. It's in the head when you are only a picture, when you only know what you say as you say it and you don't strike through. Then there's no penetration.

ELEKTRA:

When you put your cock in me it does not feel good.

PYLADES:

When I put my cock in you I want everything to go to blackness.

ELEKTRA:

It doesn't. There's always a memory that it does not feel good. Does not feel like I want it to feel. I would like to become part of what is happening and lose myself in everything. But you don't convince me.

PYLADES:

As we do it more and more, it will feel better. You'll be happier.

ELEKTRA:

Pylades, all I want to do is what's right.

PYLADES:

It is right to kill your mother. And to kill her lover Aegisthos.

ELEKTRA:

How can it be right to kill my mother or to fuck you?

PYLADES:

Blood answers blood. A parent who has killed another parent makes a tangle in the surface that we move over. The surface is no longer rolling hills, but instead it becomes riddled with caves and flames and confusions of broken forests growing on the bottoms of rivers. You know that and you feel the rottenness of it inside you. I mean you know you hate her and it should be simplified.

136

ORESTES:

Pylades is right. We know the worst that can happen is that they'll try us and we can die. But I will talk to Uncle Menelaos. He is here with Helen. Agamemnon helped Menelaos destroy Troy and recover Helen. Menelaos will defend our killing of Clytemnestra. He will be grateful to our father's memory. He'll speak for us when they put us on trial. We will get Aegisthos and mother quickly. Then we'll go to the sanctuary and stay while Menelaos speaks for us. Menelaos will want me to be king of Argos. He's my uncle.

PYLADES:

And if we die, we die.

(*To* ELEKTRA) You know I am somewhere putting myself inside of you.

(*BLACKOUT.*)

* * *

(*LIGHTS UP on* NOSTRINA *and* BASILOS.

ORESTES, ELEKTRA, PYLADES *face upstage with eyes closed.*

BASILOS *is throwing dice. He looks. Throws. Looks. Throws. Looks.*)

NOSTRINA (*carefully watching dice*):

They're all nines. (*She takes dice and rolls them.* BASILOS *looks at her roll.*)

BASILOS (*reading the roll*):

Nine. (*He takes dice back. Rolls them again.*)

137

NOSTRINA:

I know what happened.
Wait. It's going black.

BASILOS:

No. No, it isn't. Not this time. It's just a mind flicker.
You think it will and it doesn't. It's only a flitting
impression.

THYRSOS:

I don't care how long it's like this. It doesn't hurt.

NOSTRINA:

Nobody can touch them in the sanctuary after they
kill Aegisthos and Clytemnestra.

THYRSOS (*mock indifference*):

It's all politics.

(THYRSOS *swings* ORESTES *around*.
BASILOS *swings* PYLADES *around to face downstage*.
NOSTRINA *swings* ELEKTRA *around to face downstage*.)

ORESTES:

Elektra, you're here.

ELEKTRA:

I'm not. I'm somewhere else.
I'm singing.
Maybe we're killing somebody.

ORESTES:

You're here. We killed mother and uncle and now
we're in the dark. (*Looks around*.) At the back of
the temple in the old cave.
There's a fire.

138

ELEKTRA:

I don't like the smell.

ORESTES:

That's perfume. They're burning it. And feathers.
They burn feathers.

ELEKTRA:

And Pylades is here. And you are too.
Menelaos won't help us.

PYLADES:

That filthy bastard!

ELEKTRA:

So we're going to die. They want us to die for killing
mother.

ORESTES:

When we are forced to get out of here they'll kill us.
That fucking Menelaos will look pious and he'll be
regretful, but he'll be king of Argos instead of me.
And that fucking Helen, that my father killed our
little sister for, and destroyed Troy for, will be
queen of Argos alongside of our dear sweet uncle.
That cuckold grandfather Tyndareos, son of a bitch,
will be the father of the queen—just as he was the
father of the queen when our mother was there.
Look, our real grandpa was a giant white swan. He
was Leda's lover. Helen came out of an egg, and I
think—no matter what anyone says—that Clytemnestra did too. Tantalos was a son of Zeus and our
mother, like her sister Helen, was a daughter of
Zeus.
There's nothing to do.
We'll have to die.

I always told you we might have to die for this.
Pylades, I'll kill you. Then myself.

PYLADES:

No. I kill you.

ORESTES:

All right. I don't fucking care. I hate this. I'd rather
be anything than this. Something backfired.
No. I'll kill you, Pylades.
You did this for me. You joined us.

PYLADES:

It was for you and your sister.

ORESTES:

So I owe it to you. I'll kill you.

PYLADES:

Whatever you want. Whatever is easy for you.

ORESTES:

You think I'm interested in what's easy!
You son of a bitch! I care about honor! You joined
us . . .

PYLADES:

Because I love you and your sister.

ORESTES:

And you helped us in a matter of our bloodline and
godblood . . . So, I kill you!
I'LL DO YOU AND THEN I'LL DO MYSELF!

PYLADES:

All right. That's good. But do you think we're miss-
ing something? There's something we're overlook-

140

ing! Are we taking the slight way out? I mean, is this all we can do?

ORESTES:
We can't leave here, kill everyone in town, and go scot-free!

PYLADES:
We are the Furies! Aegisthos will stand there forever in a closet in eternity just as I hit him over the head with the flat of the axe. He's going to be a coward forever just as I smacked him. As long as we're *alive* it isn't closed. We shouldn't give up till we've thought of everything. Part of honor is to win.

ELEKTRA (*urgently*):
Kill me after you kill Pylades before you use the knife on yourself. I'd like it if you'd do that. Like what you did to mother when she woke up.

ORESTES:
I can't do that. You're my sister.

(*BLACKOUT.*)

* * *

(*LIGHTS UP. Scene as before.* PYLADES, ELEKTRA, ORESTES *have their eyes closed.*)

ELEKTRA:
We are in Argos.
I remember flashes.
We left the sanctuary.

141

ORESTES:

Yes. That's right.

ELEKTRA:

You and Pylades put on armor and take shields and swords and fight your way across town.

PYLADES:

Everybody who wanted entertainment came out and mobbed us and took swings. We didn't kill a single one. They got out of our way like dogs when we rushed them.
(*To* ELEKTRA.) We kept you in the middle.
You weren't hurt.

ELEKTRA:

Yes. I know it. We went to kill Aunt Helen, didn't we?
And we killed slaves, too.

ORESTES:

Yes, they're ours now. They're here.

ELEKTRA:

Are we dead? Why are we like this? Look at what we are! I don't know what we are!

PYLADES:

I was right! We'll have to go further! We'll have to kill more. This is only a half change. We must push harder.

ORESTES:

How do we push here? Where are we? It's a dream!

PYLADES:

It's a moment! It's a shattered moment we're explor-

ing. It has no duration. It is nothing but an experience as we continue our metamorphosis.
Don't panic!

ORESTES:

I never panic.
I LISTENED TO YOU!
You said when we killed mother and Aegisthos there could be a huge change. I just stood there and watched the blood coming out of her neck and she looked up at me. Her eyes went blank and stayed open and blank. Aegisthos lay there like a sack of roots—he wasn't a person any more and I knew then that nothing would happen, it was simply a deed accomplished.

PYLADES:

You were bloodhungry to do it. You were thirsty for killing them. I said I'd help you because I'm your friend.

ORESTES:

Nothing happened when we killed them!
We're like those giant black bees that hang in the air and drill into wood—we're full of energy but we don't have any thoughts.

PYLADES:

I'm thinking.

ORESTES:

That's a laugh!

PYLADES:

Helen has made a complete change. I can see it. It's a vision. We should be heroes but she made the

143

whole change and it drew energy from our transition.

ORESTES:
We've gone too far.
I can't think! I don't want to think.
I should have killed you when I met you.

(*BLACKOUT.*)

* * *

(*LIGHTS UP.* BASILOS *is dicing by himself in a spot of light.* THYRSOS *and* NOSTRINA *are lounging nearby in the darkness.*)

BASILOS (*throwing dice and reading them*):
Nine . . . Nine . . . Nine . . . Nine . . . Nine . . .
Seven . . . Seven . . . Seven . . . Nine . . .
Nine . . . Nine . . . Nine . . . Nine . . . Seven . . .
Seven . . .

NOSTRINA:
He never gets tired of it.

BASILOS (*ignoring them*):
Seven . . . Nine . . .

THYRSOS (*to* NOSTRINA):
I looked. Every throw is a four.

BASILOS (*looking up*):
That's not true.

NOSTRINA:
Let me see.

BASILOS:
No!

(BASILOS *throws dice and covers them with his hand*.)

THYRSOS:
What an old bastard!

(BASILOS *throws again and covers dice*.)

BASILOS:
Nine.

(THYRSOS *makes a gesture saying* NOSTRINA *should look herself*.)

NOSTRINA (*trying to look*):
He won't let me see.

(*Light comes up on* PYLADES.)

PYLADES:
If I could say this so you could not hear I would say something.

ORESTES (*eyes open watching from darkness*):
There's no time. This is shock.

PYLADES:
I'm a trickster-demon. That's my joy. I am death hungry. I can make us pass over into real permanence, into a heaven or a hades through shedding blood and taking lives—but not ordinary lives. They must be those who are part gods—like Helen and Clytemnestra and Aegisthos. I'll prove it as I change, and alter those around me, till there is such disturbance in the pattern of nature, till the fabric is so distraught, that huge hands battle each other

145

in a shimmering field and finally even their permanence explodes like bubbles in a wine vat. Then everything will be cancelled. I will have killed everything. I will have set it all off into dissolution and its absence will be my permanence.

ORESTES:

You're raving!
You've fucked things up!
I want my face on everything! I'll be king and it'll be that way forever. But not as a chariot, a war cart! We've got to do things over!

PYLADES:

You were hot to kill them!

ORESTES:

That's right! I like blood on my arms!

(*BLACKOUT.*)

*　*　*

(*LIGHTS UP.* HELEN *is standing in a pale light. Light on* ORESTES, ELEKTRA, PYLADES, *below.*)

HELEN (*to herself*):

Through the shell of the egg I am born in—I give off light. It is not enough!

ORESTES (*to self*):

The darkhaired slave runs from me!
Her good-looking ass!
She's out the window.
I run to Helen.
She stands there water dripping!

146

She screams.
Looks at me—mouth open and screaming.
I feel so good!
The muscles in my shoulders! Ahh!

HELEN (*self-remembering*):
Paris comes in the dark room and I give off light.
Menelaos is sleeping beside me, but Paris sees me
glowing.

(*BLACKOUT.*)

* * *

(*LIGHTS UP.*)

ORESTES:
It's pine sap smoking . . . Perfume. And feathers
burning on a sacrifice. It's all right. It's O.K. No one
can touch us. But we'll have to leave.

ELEKTRA:
We'll be weak and hungry and we'll walk out in the
light and they will kill us. The trial will be over and
they'll be waiting. They'll put us in a hole and cover
us with rocks. They'll drop the rocks on us one at a
time. We'll lie there. We'll be alive and able to
breathe a little. Sunlight will come down between
the rocks but it will never touch us. We'll groan and
we'll hear each other and it will hurt and we'll be
like that getting weaker.

PYLADES:
We're taking the slight way out. As long as we're
living, vengeance and retribution goes on and on.

While we're alive there are deaths of Clytemnestra continuing—and Aegisthos still stands with the axe-head smashing his skull, always about to fall.

ORESTES:

That's the way it should be—but there's got to be an end.

We'll walk outside and they'll do what Elektra imagines.

I'd like to get Menelaos, but that's a daydream.

He'll sit on that throne being me. Being king.

Helen will be beside him.

He's out there at the trial, being smooth, waiting for them to judge against us.

He's a traitor to his brother, my father, who led the army for him to get back Helen.

PYLADES:

There's a way. Go straight ahead, go right out of here. Beat our way through anyone who wants to stop us.

Go to Helen. Kill her.

ORESTES:

Yes!

PYLADES:

That's vengeance on Menelaos!

They'll love us for it.

She's the destroyer of Greeks and ships.

Now she's flaunting her ass here.

We'll change the valence—it will set new checks and balances. We'll not only avenge your father—we'll clean up blood debts. It's better than sitting here thinking about those bastards judging us.

We can chop her into pieces and leave a scene nobody ever dreamed of . . . The human eidolon of beauty!

With luck we can grab Hermione and have her as hostage.

We can say to let us out of the city or we kill her too. Put her to bed with her Mama Helen.

ELEKTRA:

There's been too much blood!

ORESTES:

You'll like it!

(*BLACKOUT.*)

* * *

(*LIGHTS UP.* ORESTES, PYLADES, ELEKTRA *are upstage facing upstage. Light on the* SLAVES.)

THYRSOS:

I'm good at supplicating and writhing. They're my specialty.

BASILOS:

I see it.

Their trial is going on. They are being tried for killing Aegisthos and Clytemnestra but they go to the cave—up on the hill. Back of the temple. They sit there and they can't stand it. They have kill smell in their noses. They know that Menelaos, their uncle, Helen's husband, will let them die. He won't say a word for them.

They take the old armor out of the cave . . . And they beat their way through the street from the hill to here. We can hear it going on. Hard to get this straight.

THYRSOS:
It's shock!

BASILOS:
They beat their way here. To kill Helen.

THYRSOS:
Pylades! It's his idea.

BASILOS:
He's an ideologue. Now I work for him—he's my boss. Worse than Helen. She's only obsessed with herself. He wants to kill to make changes. He wants to kill gods to make gods—and bring everything down. To bring everything to a cold-blooded stop. He thinks nothingness is his monument, that if he kills enough it becomes real—then there's even more deaths and it flies apart. Into nothingness! It's crazy. Everything cancels everything out.

(*BLACKOUT.*)

* * *

(*LIGHTS UP.* NOSTRINA *is working at her wound trying to tie a cord around the stump of her arm under her blouse.*)

NOSTRINA:
Help me.

150

THYRSOS:

Bitch! If we were going to die we'd be dead by now.

(*Light on* ORESTES *and* ELEKTRA. *They speak as children. They are moved by* NOSTRINA *and* THYRSOS *as they speak.*)

ORESTES:

When you drink, you must give wine to the black gods—Chthonic Pluto, and Dis, and Persephone— so they won't change things and make everything different. (*He spits imaginary wine onto floor.*) There! (*Spits again.*) You must do it three times. (*He spits wine.*) There!

ELEKTRA:

You don't do that! You pour it. Like this. And like this. Like this.

ORESTES:

I stand in the ashes and smell the smoke. Like the smell on men's clothes when they come back. That makes me know what to do. I know there's a big world with sounds of swords hitting things, and horses, and things burning. And laughing. There are yells. (*Pause.*) They went to Troy to get Aunt Helen.

(*Light on* HELEN *standing. Light is coming out of* HELEN.)

HELEN:

The light comes from me and I am what I always am and less. It is not enough to be in the sky and give off light. To always be memories giving off light is Hell. Here in the sky is Hades.
God blood trickles from me like gold and silver.

151

They know that to be so beautiful is to be more than human. I am more than a star—to be a star is not enough!

This is not worthy of my beauty.

I am gentler and greater and more lovely than this.

Better to be in blackness than only be a star. I can do much more.

The radiance I give off is chains.

The old men drool and look at me. They know I am more.

Someone is always coming with swords and cocks. I am not a cold star. I am meant to be a goddess.

I have so much to do to make penetration.

(*BLACKOUT.*)

* * *

(*Lights up on* BASILOS, THYRSOS, NOSTRINA.)

THYRSOS (*listening, indicating with his head*):
 What are those?

BASILOS:
 Wild dogs barking. Crickets.

THYRSOS (*smoothing legs*):
 I wonder if I'll be able to shave.

NOSTRINA (*pointing to* ORESTES):
 When Orestes chopped off my arm he shouted: THIS IS FOR MY SISTER ELEKTRA!

BASILOS:
 So you're her servant.

152

(*Light on* ELEKTRA.)

ELEKTRA (*to* NOSTRINA):
Swing me around.

(NOSTRINA *swings* ELEKTRA *around*.)

ELEKTRA:
We are on the boat and there is a wind that makes
the sails flap. A loud sound. We go back on the boat
because there is wind.
There are gulls, they land on the boat.
I am a baby and I remember. I remember the sound
and the slave girl who carries me and puts me in
Mama's arms.
I am a baby and I see. The priest does it. He cuts
my sister's throat like she is a sheep. I don't know it
is real. It is nice that the red runs out of her throat.
Everyone yells. They like it. They shout. The priest
sings. He hands my sister to Agamemnon. His face
is big.
There's a wind. I remember the boat.

(*BLACKOUT.*)

* * *

(*LIGHTS UP. Lights on* ORESTES *and* PYLADES.
Scene begins slow and then moves like a dance.
ORESTES *and* PYLADES *are moved in their chariots.*)

ORESTES:
No!
I've lost it.
Can't think. Can't feel.

153

PYLADES:

It's shock. We're heads made out of wood.
I hit the one with the beard. A smash in the skull.
It doesn't hurt. One smash in the head.
Clean.

ORESTES:

I take the arm off the girl. Kill for Elektra.
I yell it's for her when I make the kill.
That makes it solid. Like a kid game.
I yell.
Then it goes black.

(*BLACKOUT.*)

* * *

(*LIGHTS UP. Scene begins slow and then moves like a dance. ORESTES and PYLADES are moved in their chariots.*)

PYLADES:

We chop her up.
I'm a bird with black wings. I fly into the change.
We shape the stuff of matter. We're killing a person who's more than half god.
It's a rapture. Carved out of matter. Not heavenly stuff. Not some dream of just voices.
The real thing.
We chop her up.

ORESTES:

I get her first. She screams. Water shooting out of her eyes.
She's only meat.

154

She's a book about surgery.
Butchery.
She falls down. Pylades hits her again. That knocks
her straight.

PYLADES:

I'm in a big empty space.
The muscles of my arms.
I'm in my lungs.

                She falls to the left and Orestes hits
her.

ORESTES:

Then we're here.

          We're the history of information.
       We're bound by our acts into sculpture.
Can't break out.

                Smashed by the gesture!

PYLADES:

Hit her an upward blow!

             She stands straight.
       Piece off her shoulder!

ORESTES:

On the floor.

              Chop off the hand. The foot.

PYLADES:

Now!

ORESTES:

     Gore over everything.
Shining guts.

               Black streaks in the air.
They love me again!
They make me king.

Killing the murderess of cities.

PYLADES:
In shock.
All changed to violent nature.
It's all my empty tomb with no walls. Only real pic-
tures of nothing going on.
Then no nothing!
Not even nothing!

BASILOS:
It's shock.

ORESTES:
But the actions are armor!
There's no penetration.
We're the immobile body of it all.
Freedom makes us nothing!

PYLADES:
Hermione!

ELEKTRA:
Here's a basket.
Push her in there.
She's all slushed in Helen's blood.
SHE SMELLS LIKE SHIT!
Push her in the pool!

BASILOS (*loud, but matter-of-fact, and spoken over the above speeches*):
His eyes so bloodshot they are scarlet. A boar hog's eyes. He runs at me as hard as he can and he swings it. He swings it . . . My head explodes before it hits me. When it hits I don't feel a thing. His eyes so bloodshot they are scarlet. A boar hog's eyes . . .

156

(*BLACKOUT.*)

* * *

(*Lights up on* HELEN.)

HELEN:

Only as a goddess am I free—can I cut it away! I'm blocked and hang as a star to be loved and hated. I must change it! Change the fabric. Make everything whole. As a goddess I reach into nature and take up Troy and smooth it with my fingers amd make it whole. I raise up the city and the bodies of soldiers. I MUST DO THAT! I will smooth away remembrance of the war. The war will cease to exist! There will be singing and feasting. They will all love me for my beauty and kindness. There will be no death! Every man I've loved will be one man. Paris and Menelaos will be joined in one man. There'll be no jealousy! Every woman any man has ever loved will be one woman. There'll be no murder or hate or jealousy. I'm a goddess! AND I REACH FOR THAT! It will be a vision of grapes that hang in the orange and blue and black sunset, while children's voices sing hymns . . . I'LL SMOOTH AWAY THE REMEMBRANCE OF WAR.
THE WAR WILL CEASE TO EX-IST!   THERE WILL BE SINGING AND FEASTING.   THEY WILL ALL LOVE ME FOR MY BEAUTY AND KIND-NESS.   THERE WILL BE NO DEATH!   EVERY MAN I'VE

LOVED WILL
    BE ONE MAN.
        PARIS AND ME-
NELAOS WILL BE JOINED IN ONE MAN.
THERE'LL BE NO JEALOUSY!
    EVERY WOMAN ANY MAN
      HAS LOVED WILL BE ONE
WOMAN.
    THERE'LL BE NO MURDER
OR HATE OR WAR OR JEALOUSY.
I'M A GODDESS!
I REACH FOR THAT!
IT WILL BE A VISION OF GRAPES THAT
HANG IN THE ORANGE AND BLUE AND
BLACK SUNSET WHILE CHILDREN'S
VOICES SING HYMNS . . . I'LL . . .

PYLADES (*SHOUTING*):
 GODDAMN YOU! DIE! BE DEAD!

BASILOS:
 SEVEN! (*Throws dice.*) SEVEN!

 (*BLACKOUT.*)

     *   *   *

 (*During blackout* BASILOS *throws dice in darkness.*)

BASILOS:
 Seven . . . Seven . . . Seven . . .

 (*LIGHTS UP.* BASILOS *is dicing.* ORESTES, ELEK-

TRA, PYLADES *placed as in scene one.* BASILOS,
NOSTRINA, THYRSOS *placed as in scene one.*)

BASILOS:
Seven . . . Seven . . .

THYRSOS (*without looking at dice*):
I don't believe it!

BASILOS (*throwing*):
Three . . . Three . . . Three . . . (*Throws and
pauses and looks at* THYRSOS.)

THYRSOS:
Let me guess. Three?

(NOSTRINA *is working at her wound trying to tie a
cord around the stump of her arm under the
blouse.*)

NOSTRINA:
Help me.

THYRSOS:
Bitch! If we were going to die we'd be dead.

NOSTRINA:
There, I stopped the blood again. (*Looks around.*) I
never thought it would be like this.

THYRSOS:
It is. (*Listens. Tosses head.*) What are those?

BASILOS:
Wild dogs barking. Crickets.

THYRSOS:
This must be the end.

BASILOS:
    Or the beginning. (*Throws*.) Seven.

NOSTRINA:
    It's going black.

    (*BLACKOUT.*)

                        *   *   *

    (*Lights flicker up*.)

BASILOS:
    Seven . . .

    (*BLACKOUT.*)

                        *   *   *

    (*Lights flicker up*.)

BASILOS:
    Seven . . .

    (*BLACKOUT.*)

Selected Grove Press Theater Paperbacks

17061-X ARDEN, JOHN / John Arden Plays: One (Sergeant Musgrave's Dance, The Workhouse Donkey, Armstrong's Last Goodnight) / $4.95

17213-2 ARTAUD, ANTONIN / The Theater and Its Double / $4.95

17083-0 AYCKBOURN, ALAN / Absurd Person Singular, Absent Friends, Bedroom Farce: Three Plays / $3.95

17253-1 BARAKA, IMAMU AMIRI (LEROI JONES) / The Baptism and The Toilet: Two Plays / $3.95

17900-5 BARAKA, IMAMU AMIRI (LEROI JONES) / The System of Dante's Hell, The Dead Lecturer and Tales / $4.95

62410-6 BASSNETT-McGUIRE, SUSAN / Luigi Pirandello / $9.95

17208-6 BECKETT, SAMUEL / Endgame / $2.95

17233-7 BECKETT, SAMUEL / Happy Days / $2.95

62061-5 BECKETT, SAMUEL / Ohio Impromptu, Catastrophe, What Where: Three Plays / $4.95

17924-2 BECKETT, SAMUEL / Rockaby and Other Works / $3.95

17204-3 BECKETT, SAMUEL / Waiting for Godot / $3.50 [See also Nine plays of the Modern Theater, Harold Clurman, ed., 17411-9 / $11.95]

17052-0 BEHAN, BRENDAN / The Complete Plays (The Hostage, The Quare Fellow, Richard's Cork Leg, Three One Act Plays for Radio) / $8.95

17932-3 BENTLEY, ERIC / Are You Now Or Have You Ever Been and Other Plays (The Recantation of Galileo Galilei; From the Memoirs of Pontius Pilate) / $12.50

17734-7 BENTLEY, ERIC / The Brecht Commentaries / $9.50

62418-1 BERLIN, NORMAND / Eugene O'Neill / $9.95

17258-2 BRECHT, BERTOLT / The Caucasian Chalk Circle / $2.95

17111-X BRECHT, BERTOLT / Edward II: A Chronicle Play / $1.95

17112-8 BRECHT, BERTOLT / Galileo / $2.95

17109-8 BRECHT, BERTOLT / The Good Woman of Setzuan / $2.95

17100-4 BRECHT, BERTOLT / The Jewish Wife and Other Short Plays (In Search of Justice, The Informer, The Elephant Calf, The Measures Taken, The Exception and the Rule, Salzburg Dance of Death) / $2.95

17065-2 BRECHT, BERTOLT / The Mother / $2.95

17226-4   IONESCO, EUGENE / Rhinoceros and Other Plays (The Leader, The Future Is in Eggs) / $4.95

17311-2   IONESCO, EUGENE / A Stroll in the Air and Frenzy for Two or More: Two Plays / $2.45

17485-2   JARRY, ALFRED / The Ubu Plays (Ubu Rex, Ubu Cuckolded, Ubu Enchained) / $9.95

17744-4   KAUFMAN, GEORGE, and HART, MOSS / Three Plays (Once in A Lifetime; You Can't Take It With You; The Man Who Came to Dinner) / $6.95

62411-4   LYONS, CHARLES / Samuel Beckett / $9.95

17016-4   MAMET, DAVID / American Buffalo / $4.95

62049-6   MAMET, DAVID / Glengarry Glen Ross / $6.95

17040-7   MAMET, DAVID / A Life in the Theatre / $3.95

17043-1   MAMET, DAVID / Sexual Perversity in Chicago and The Duck Variations: Two Plays / $3.95

17062-8   MAMET, DAVID / The Water Engine and Mr. Happiness: Two Plays / $3.95

17105-5   MOON, SAMUEL, ed. / One Act: Eleven Short Plays of the Modern Theater (Miss Julie by August Strindberg, Purgatory by William Butler Yeats, The Man With the Flower in His Mouth by Luigi Pirandello, Pullman Car Hiawatha by Thornton Wilder, Hello Out There by William Saroyan, 27 Wagons Full of Cotton by Tennessee Williams, Bedtime Story by Sean O'Casey, Cecile by Jean Anouilh, This Music Crept By Me Upon the Waters by Archibald MacLeish, A Memory of Two Mondays by Arthur Miller, The Chairs by Eugene Ionesco) / $7.95

17264-7   MROZEK, SLAWOMIR / Striptease, Tango, Vatzlav: Three Plays / $12.50

17092-X   ODETS, CLIFFORD / Six Plays of Clifford Odets (Waiting for Lefty, Awake and Sing, Golden Boy, Rocket to the Moon, Till the Day I Die, Paradise Lost) / $7.95

17001-6   ORTON, JOE / The Complete Plays (The Ruffian on the Stair, The Good and Faithful Servant, The Erpingham Camp, Funeral Games, Loot, What the Butler Saw, Entertaining Mr. Sloane) / $6.95

17084-9   PINTER, HAROLD / Betrayal / $3.95

17232-9   PINTER, HAROLD / The Birthday Party and The Room: Two Plays / $4.95

17019-9   PINTER, HAROLD / Complete Works: One (The Birthday Party, The Room, The Dumb Waiter, A Slight Ache, A Night Out, The Black and White, The Examination) / $6.95

17020-2   PINTER, HAROLD / Complete Works: Two (The Caretaker, Night School, The Dwarfs, The Collection, The Lover, Five Revue Sketches) / $6.95

17051-2 PINTER, HAROLD / Complete Works: Three (Landscape Silence, The Basement, Six Revue Sketches, Tea Party [play], Tea Party [short story], Mac) $6.95
17251-5 PINTER, HAROLD / The Homecoming / $4.95
17675-8 PINTER, HAROLD / The Hothouse / $4.95
17539-5 POMERANCE, BERNARD / The Elephant Man / $4.25
17743-6 RATTIGAN, TERENCE / Plays: One (French Without Tears; The Winslow Boy; The Browning Version; Harlequinade) / $5.95
17084-9 PINTER, HAROLD / Betrayal / $3.95
17232-9 PINTER, HAROLD / The Birthday Party and The Room: Two Plays / $4.95
17019-9 PINTER, HAROLD / Complete Works: One (The Birthday Party, The Room, The Dumb Waiter, A Slight Ache, A Night Out, The Black and White, The Examination) / $6.95
17020-2 PINTER, HAROLD / Complete Works: Two (The Caretaker, Night School, The Dwarfs, The Collection, The Lover, Five Revue Sketches) / $6.95
17051-2 PINTER, HAROLD / Complete Works: Three (Landscape Silence, The Basement, Six Revue Sketches, Tea Party [play], Tea Party [short story], Mac) $6.95
17251-5 PINTER, HAROLD / The Homecoming / $4.95
17675-8 PINTER, HAROLD / The Hothouse / $4.95
17539-5 POMERANCE, BERNARD / The Elephant Man / $4.25
17743-6 RATTIGAN, TERENCE / Plays: One (French Without Tears; The Winslow Boy; The Browning Version; Harlequinade) / $5.95
62040-2 SETO, JUDITH ROBERTS / The Young Actor's Workbook / $8.95
17661-8 SHAWN, WALLACE / Marie and Bruce / $4.95
17948-X SHAWN, WALLACE, and GREGORY, ANDRÉ / My Dinner with André / $5.95
17866-1 STOPPARD, TOM / Jumpers / $2.95
17085-7 STOPPARD, TOM / Night and Day / $3.95
17260-4 STOPPARD, TOM / Rosencrantz and Guildenstern Are Dead / $3.95
17884-X STOPPARD, TOM / Travesties / $3.95
17206-X WALEY, ARTHUR, tr. and ed. / The Nō Plays of Japan / $5.95
62499-8 WHITAKER, THOMAS / Tom Stoppard / $9.95

Available from your local bookstore, or directly from Grove Press. (Add $1.00 postage and handling for the first book and 50¢ for each additional book.)

GROVE PRESS, INC., 196 West Houston St., New York, N.Y. 10014